Lord of the Mountain

The Sardiel Poems

by

Rienzi Crusz

We acknowledge the support of the Canada Council for the Arts for our publishing program. We also acknowledge support from the Ontario Arts Council.

First published

TSAR Publications, Toronto, ON, Canada, 1999

Author photograph by Jerome Crusz.

ELVIN HILL
PUBLISHING

Second edition
Elvin Hill Publishing,
166 MacGregor Crescent
Waterloo, ON, Canada
N2J 3X3

ISBN 0-920661-82-3
Cover design by Michael Crusz
Printed at Pandora Press
33 Kent Ave.
Kitchener, Ont

ALSO BY RIENZI CRUSZ:

Flesh and Thorn
Elephant and Ice
Singing Against the Wind
A Time for Loving
Still Close to the Raven
The Rain Doesn't Know Me Any More
Beatitudes of Ice
Insurgent Rain (TSAR Book)

CRITICAL PRAISE FOR RIENZI CRUSZ'S POETRY:

If you want to share a sensibility which is at once primitive and sophisticated, both intense and subtle, a poetic craft which is taut and concentrated, then read *Flesh and Thorn*.   *Quarry*

Can Lit . . . has never articulated and transcended the experience of the incomer so wonderfully . . . the voice rings with a timbre known at once and altogether distinct; its range is abnormally large; its tone of infinite variety.   *The New Quarterly*

The cultural gift Crusz offers us, as a kind of magnificent verbal embroidery of the plain cloth of Canadian speech, continually surprises, delights, mystifies and liberates those of us raised on the sound of what Northrop Fry has called "the Canadian goose honk."
      The Toronto South Asian Review

Arguably the best living Sri Lankan poet in English, though he has been in Canada since 1965, Crusz belongs to that older post-colonial generation, including such writers as Walcott and Soyinka, prepared to appropriate the colonial legacy of Shakespeare and English without anguished breast beating, "as a tongue to speak with."   *World Literature Today*

His "Immigrant's Song" is not only an attempt to come to terms with his own past, it is also a heroic statement of poetic independence.   Arun Mukherjee, *Currents*

Crusz, the most delicately nuanced (of such voices) uses his to balance a history, a role, and a difficult displacement . . . Like the West Indian poet, Derek Walcott [he] will not indulge in simplified opposition, whether of language, culture or colour. *Ariel*

Crusz's language is subtle and he makes his points obliquely. Moreover, his self-examination always includes the social context of an immigrant's struggle for a sense of identity. *Books in Canada*

The Sun-Man poems are major artifacts of a new Canadian sensibility, important for the realities of our national selfhood.
Nancy Lou Patterson, University of Waterloo

Here was a true poetry of the displaced self, with sorrow beneath its bemused surface. Opposites—elephant and ice—are reconciled by a delightful wit, and ferocious though may be his interior heat, the light that the Sun-Man sheds upon the world lingers in the mind with a lovely after-glow.
Zulfikar Ghose, University of Texas

To call Crusz an immigrant poet is to summarize his intents too glibly. In both his books it is not the obvious contrast between elephant and ice, Sri Lanka and Canada, that is central but rather the manifold and specific ways in which a certain sensibility tries to cope honestly with perennial themes in both cultures.
Reshard Gool

A most articulate poetry, with a fascinating sense of where you come from and where to.   Robert Creely

His real genius lies not in the message contained in the poetry, but in the pursuit of perfection in poetic form. Very much a poet of sound and rhythm, Crusz writes with an awareness that poetry is about language, about the power of imagination. He is a very self-conscious poet, and that is precisely why his reputation will outlast that of his contemporaries.
Chelva Kanaganayakam, University of Toronto

ACKNOWLEDGEMENTS

Some of these poems first appeared in *The Wascana Review, The Toronto Review, Fiddlehead, Insurgent Rain: Selected Poems 1974-1996; Still Close to the Raven* (TSAR, 1989); *The Rain Doesn't Know Me Any More* (TSAR, 1992); *Beatitudes of Ice* (TSAR, 1995).

I thank the Canada Council and the Ontario Arts Council for their financial assistance in writing this book.

My special thanks to all those who helped me in this project, especially to Stephen Heighton and Chelva Kanaganayakam for their early encouragement; and to the following for their invaluable suggestions and editorial advice: Barry Dempster, Richard Harrison, Michael Thorpe, Andrew Stubbs, Don Gutteridge, James Panabaker, Victor Ramraj, and Shyamal and Sumana Bagchee. I am solely responsible for any shortcomings that may be in this work.

AUTHOR'S NOTE

The legend of the Sri Lankan outlaw Sardiel has been told and retold in several official Sri Lankan documents, books and newpaper articles and on film. This work attempts to recast the Sardiel story as a montage of prose and poetry. The passionate temperament of Sardiel and his times provides some justification for this literary departure.

Legends die hard. Revising a figure of legend, a cultural icon, and searching for the man behind the myth is always a challenge. Revisionist interpretations, however, in whatever form, rarely sit well with those whose nationalist feelings admit no new perspectives on their heroes. If, in my reading, Sardiel emerges as a flawed and paradoxical character, then his legend, it would seem to me, far from being diminished, has simply regained the patina of humanity.

While I have generally kept to the basic facts of the Sardiel story, inventions of circumstance and detail have been used when deemed necessary by the dynamic of fiction and idioms of poetry.

Rienzi Crusz

This book
has always been for HENRY
that other beloved rebel

Contents

And so I danced in a circle of blood,
    wondering about my life,
the cruel shadows of Uttuwankande's Rock,
        God's flagrant mistake, the karma
of all these things

SARDIEL

Prologue

THE EXECUTION

The white caps were then pulled over their faces, the two executioners and the Moorish priest descending leaving the two who were so to be launched into eternity; and the Roman Catholic priest praying for Sardiel.

Everything being reported to Mr Templer as ready, he, having his back towards the scene the whole time, momentarily turned round to see that it was so, gave the signal; the bolt was withdrawn and both dropped leaving the priest who had firm hold of the railing on the top.The poor wretches did not appear to struggle, but now and then from muscular efforts their hands would rise and drop with sudden jerks and in a few minutes all was still.

Sardiel died as he was beginning to say the "Our Father" (in Sinhalese) " but his soul I am sure ended this sublime prayer in heaven." (Fr Duffo)

About half past 9 their bodies were cut down and put into coffins and carried into a cart drawn by convicts to the burial grounds by the Katoogastota road outside of which their bodies were buried and by 10 o'clock the gallows were taken down and all traces of the two murderers effaced.

The Examiner (Colombo), 11 May 1864

3

E L E G Y

> . . . the true revolutionary is guided
> by great feelings of love
>   CHE GUEVARA

We heard the swish and crack
of the hanging ropes,
the thud of your falling body—
dead. You are not dead, Sardiel;
the oil lamps on this rugged Uttuwankande peak
still sing your precious song, the karma
of its pith and purpose.

The Englishman will no doubt write your epitaph
with gunpowder in his soul:
"Here lies Sardiel, the rebellious bandit,
dead as a dog. Hail Britannia, Hail!"

Ours,
bred in the bone of this blessed land,
will lay bare his fictions,
his bloody knuckles of empire,
as history stands by with lowered eyes,
and the hound of time comes to rest
with the truth between its teeth.

We ask, as you once did,
the same questions:
Who ravaged whom?
Who's the victim, who's the bandit?
Who the conqueror, who the damned?

Did *they* fashion *your* sacrificial altars,
drive the necessary lambs

into your arms, the deaths
of Sabhan, Nasurdeen, van Haught,
Christain Appu, the *chettiar*, the Arab?

Or do we hear
an argument of birth, a destiny,
a dharma writ large in blood?
What happened to *ahimsa*,
that gentleness that ruled your mother's life
like a habit?
Whose map led you nowhere
but to the hanging tree?

Show me, Sardiel,
the underbelly of your soul,
and tell me
it wasn't you, you,
with an ego huge as elephant
pounding a bloody trail
after the phantom of fame?

And the karma of blood?
You say: ask the Englishman
who, masked
in civilization,
rushed these cinnamon shores,
caught the green land between his locust teeth
and took it all
in gunsmoke, the hell
of his dark soul.

Sardiel,
we still hear the sacrificial bleating
like an ardent song for your cause:
the poor, the poor, the poor;
the sight, the sound, the smell of freedom;

the sunlight on the bright red coffee seeds
dancing on your mother's small palms.

Be still, noble spirit.

chettiar: money-lender
ahimsa: Buddhist theory of gentleness

In the Beginning

A HOUSE DIVIDED

Father Time and Mother Earth,
a marriage on the rocks . . .
        JAMES MERRILL

Molligoda, Kadugannawa. Village
of bright coffee, new love, the first born—
Sardiel suckling at his mother's breasts,
as father Adarsi Appu sips his fermenting joy,
arrack, roasted cashew nuts,
his *beedi's* dim glow,
dark curl of smoke.

No sudden streak of ungodly light,
no clouds on fire, no blue moon,
only a raven's persistent squawk,
the distant peel of Temple bells
to herald this birth.

Then, to Haldanduwana, ancestral home—
and four siblings: Peduru, Gabriel, Anthony, Martha.
Sweet swirl of childhood. Memories.
Warm as the morning sun, bountiful
as mother Pinchohami's breakfast table—
hoppers and *seeni-sambol.*

Where Sardiel captains the *gudu* games,
and little Martha, lovingly tolerated,
plays with the boys.
Restless joy   the mora-fruit raids,
wicker baskets   bright red coffee seeds,
the banana grove at the mercy
of five pairs of small grabbing hands.
How Sardiel climbs the backyard jak tree

and a sun-ripe fruit
rides down slowly at the end of a rope
to Martha and her impatient brothers
squatting by the tree's huge feet.

Time's cruel harvest:
life's broken journeys, sad exits.
Karma's absolute destinies.
Pinchohami returns to Kadugannawa
with Martha and Sardiel.
He, to the Beligammana Temple School,
she, at home with pots and pans,
mother's rice pot crying through its steam.

Where the two children learn the Buddha's way—
Bodhi Puja, evening *bana*,
the sacred bo tree
with a hundred oil lamps flickering
at its feet;
Vesak lanterns, the joyous *rabana* beat,
ahimsa, *nibbhana*, Buddha's words
falling like manna from their mothers' lips,
the Temple monks.

A house now divided.
Adarsi stays behind, clings
to his ancestral home, his children
Peduru, Gabriel and Anthony.
A sudden journey, a pilgrimage of fate.

His bullock cart rumbles
over a long winding dirt road
as the tired bulls fuss and heave,
froth at the mouth.
On to Talawila, St Anne's Church.
There, after the festive High Mass,

Adarsi and the children embrace
their Christian God, their separate path.

A tired unforgiving father
gazes through a church window—
a forked road, a lost love
an absent son
with a heart of darkness.

beedi: small, rolled cigarette
Vesak: festival of Buddha's birth in spring
gudu: village sport played with two sticks
bana: Buddhist reading from the scriptures and sermon
rabana: a large drum for festive occasions, usually played by women
ahimsa: theory of gentleness in Buddhist philosophy
nibbhana: state of enlightenment

BEGINNING OF THE END

Temple school playground.

One little *vaysige putha,*
two little *vaysige puthas,*
three little *vaysige puthas*

showing off
gold *havadiyas* round
their fat waists,
silk sarongs catching
the mercury of the sun,

laughing   jeering—
as noon's searching light

picks holes
in my gauze banian, the mud
on my cotton sarong.

Their fathers
sucking up to the *Suddhas*
and growing fat
on the poor of the land.

And I'll say it again:
"One little son-of-a-bitch,
two little sons-of-bitches,
three little sons-of-bitches,

some day, some day,
I'll . . . "

havadiya: gold chain worn round the waist
vaysige putha: son-of-a-bitch
Suddha: Englishman, white man

PEDURU TO AMMA

Dearest *Amma,*

I need your help. Something's wrong with Sardiel *aiya.* I am
sending you this note through *nangi,* so Sardiel *aiya* , who is
always behind and before me and has the ears of an
elephant, won't know. When you and father arranged to put
aiya and me in the Illukgoda Temple School, I was excited.
Not so, *aiya.* Something's wrong with him.

Yesterday, the temple monk spoke to us about good and evil.
What karma means. He said that the *aratchi's* and headman's
children, who were given prominent places at the head of the
class, were rich and well fed because of the meritorious
deeds in their previous lives. Pointing to us, he then said:
"Look at Adardsi Appu's children. They are poor, half-
starved, and shabbily clad." When he asked Sardiel
why that was so, brother got very angry. He did not answer.
I saw his fists clench, his jaws tighten, and his face go red at
the temples. He then turned to me and muttered: " Damn
karma. I'll show the *vaysige puthas* how to change all that."

Amma, I am scared. I don't know what Sardiel *aiya* will do.
To make things worse, the rich boys in the class overheard
brother's threats and decided to teach *aiya* a lesson.They'd
give him a good thrashing. I pleaded with him to come
home, but he wouldn't listen.

For a while I hid behind a big rock to see what would hap-
pen. The *aratchi's* and headman's sons circled round Sardiel
aiya with wicked sneers on their faces and they fought. The
last thing I saw before I ran home was brother's clenched
fists flailing wildly in the air.

Speak to him, *Amma,* before he falls into dangerous and evil
ways. Maybe father could explain to him the dangers of his
uncontrolled temper. I am now wondering whether these
strange attitudes of Sardiel will lead to an end of my own

schooling.

Love,
    Peduru

amma: mother
nangi : younger sister
aiya: elder brother
aratchi: village official
vaysige putha: son-of-a-bitch

MOTHER AND DAUGHTER: KITCHEN TALK

She's on her haunches blowing hard into damp firewood
to keep the fire going.
The pot of rice will soon be done. Yesterday's dry-fish curry
should be enough for two.
Father Adarsi Appu is away in Peradeniya selling tobacco.

"*Amma*, where's Sardiel *aiya?*"

"Who knows? Perhaps, rolling dice with his friends
in his mountain cave.
Or swatting mosquitoes and sharing venison and rainwater
with his gang in some far patch of jungle "

"You know, *Amma*, now I remember.
One afternoon, I saw Sardiel *aiya* cutting up a *gemba* limb by

and carefully smashing each limb with a big rock stone.
When I asked him if Lord Budddha would bless him

for such a cruel act, he flew into a rage and shouted :

'Shut up, *nangi*, do you know how many innocent flies
have died today in the *gemba's* big mouth?
The fly did nothing to *gemba*, but *gemba* was so damn proud
of the power in his big jaws—what do you want me to do?
Wait for Lord Buddha to come down and save little fly's life?"

gemba : frog
aiya: elder brother
nangi: younger sister
amma: mother

INTERLUDE: BY MENAKA'S WELL

With the silence of a cat
he's behind her,
a Temple flower in his right hand:
"Love me, Menaka, love me."
She smiles and looks away.

"Love me, Menaka, love me,"
he pleads again,
    but her eyes are nowhere
as she lowers her bucket into the well,

for the teapot's waiting,
    the rice pot, her mother's weary bones;
    "Love me, Menaka, love me "
he begs once more,

his head a whirlpool of hot blood.

She looks deep into his searching eyes:
"*Anay,* Sardiel *aiya,* I can't.
You are the wind,
   here now and gone like the raven;

how your heart leaps
   when the sun is high
and I'm in the pathway of your eyes,
   but how it falters and falls

when night invites a raging moon,
   a storm of fireflies,
the smell of toddy   friends
   their embracing laughter,
the music in the rolling dice."

anay: an exclamation of pain
aiya: elder brother

MOTHER AND DAUGHTER #2

"Amma, Amma, quietly steal into the back yard and look over
the hedge. Sardiel *aiya,* Peduru, Gabriel, and Antony are
breaking Lord Buddha's teachings.

"Sardiel has made a noose of coconut-leaf spine to catch the
garden lizards. Gabriel and Peduru are laughing at his
nadagam. When brother Sardiel had noosed a small blood-
red *katussa,* he broke one of its front legs and said: 'Now run,
you pariah, run!' The poor creature hobbled a few feet side-
ways. Brother then caught the *katussa* again, cut off his right
hind leg with his penknife and taunted him once more:
'Now run, you pariah, run!' The poor creature could now
hardly move, but it struggled valiantly to do so. Sardiel
stabbed its left eye. Finally, he turned the poor animal on its
belly and shouted: 'You coward, you deserve what you're get-
ting. How many times did you throw out your long raspy
tongue and suck in the innocent butterflies that were only
enjoying their brief lives in the sun!'

"*Amma,* brother was about to noose another innocent *katussa,*
when I ran up to him and screamed into his sweating face:

" 'Stop it, *aiya,* stop it! What do you think you're doing? The
katussa is as innocent as the butterfly. It's only doing what
it knows to do. Didn't the Temple monks teach us not to hurt
any creature, even an ant? So stop this cruel game of yours!'

"At this, brother got angry and screamed back : 'Shut up,
Martha, what do you know of innocence and guilt? You who
hang on to *Amma's redda* like a leech and know nothing of the
world beyond the banana trees in our backyard.The *katussa* is
only innocent so long as it keeps its innocence. The moment
it hurts the butterfly, it's guilty! To me, the *katussa* is another
shape for the *Suddhas,* the bloody English, who have taken
our lands and swallowed our lives. Remember that, girl.'

"What is wrong with him, *Amma*? What did he learn from
the *pansala* priests at Illukgoda? Maybe you should get a

kattadiya to drive the devil out of him. I hope in the Lord Buddha's name that his younger brothers do not fall into his wicked ways."

amma: mother
aiya: elder brother
katussa: garden lizard
pansala: Buddhist Temple
ahimsa: Buddhist theory of gentleness
kattadiya: devil dancer who drives out evil spirits
redda: sarong-like garment
nadagam: foolery

BLACK MAGIC

Slumped lazily against the thick trunk of a goraka tree, Sardiel takes another deep draw on his *beedi*. No qualms of conscience here. Smoking the pungent *beedi* is the favourite and conventional sin of adolescence. Besides, life is one great bore, and tending to Mr Samarasinghe's cattle is hardly the job to match his fourteen-year-old restless and rudderless spirit. His mind is on the "Rock"—The Rock of Uttu-wankande, which looms dark and forbidding over him. He *must* climb it, unearth its secrets.

So the cowherd deserts the cattle for the mountain dream.

A pelting sun is now Sardiel's cruel and only companion for the climb. Thick sweat collects on his face, salts his mouth; bruised knees smudge blood on his sarong, show through tatters over his thighs. Mercifully, the sun begins to desert the mountain and sinks into its twilight sleep. He climbs on.

Reaching the top, marked by a cairn of rocks, he clambers

up, throws out his arms to the evening sky and shouts to the
valley below: *I am Sardiel, Lord of Uttuwankande!* A passing
crow, velvet black by evening light, squawks a loud: AMEN!
His elation wanes and Sardiel sits down to rest by a pile of
stones, smoke another *beedi.* As the beedi smoke curls up and
away into the thick air, in those moments of fading light,
when shadows dance and shift, playing games with the eyes,
he catches sight of something that seems like the leaves of a
book amid the clutter of rocks. A strange feeling comes over
him as he holds the book in his dirty hands. It's old, very old,
an ola-leaf book that seems strange and valuable. But he can-
not make out the words.

Yet he suspects that his life, his fate, is connected with the
mysterious writing. Tucking his treasure safely under his
shirt, Sardiel begins to scramble down the mountain.

A few days later. The village of Dikkobupitiya. An *abitiya*
greets a ragged pilgrim at the gates of the Temple. The young
pilgrim, clutching his precious book, requests to meet the old
monk, whom he has learnt is an authority on antiquarian
books and magic. Ushered in, he's before a hunched old man
with a few short white hairs on his otherwise bald head; his
hands shake with the palsy, but his eyes are as black and
piercing as in his youth.

"What, what, *lamaya?* Speak up. Don't waste my time!"

There is a marked rudeness in his voice, an impatience so
common to some gifted men.

"*Hamuduruwane*, this ola-leaf book," begins Sardiel with a
touch of frightened hesitancy in his voice. "I found it on the
top of the Rock of Uttuwankande. What does it say? I cannot
read the writing.What does it mean?"

No sooner has the book passed into the old monk's hands
than their tremors subside. His eyes strain and widen, focus-
ing intently on the tattered pages. He then begins to chant in
a slow quavering voice the words inscribed on the ola leaves.
Goes on and on, the chant becoming much like the temple rit-

ual of *seth kavi,* until he turns over the final page.

"Sit down, *lamaya* .What you have here is a book of magic, an heirloom of some great magician. It's an invaluable treasure if you learn to master its secrets. Whoever recites its *mantarams* will have the power to change his form at will to keep out the cold reaching hand of death. Since you have traveled so far, I am prepared to teach you the *mantarams* in three days, if you so wish"

Sardiel nods and smiles. It's an explosive smile, a smile that says, "*Buddhu Ammo,* I now have the key to my destiny, the code to my karma." He stays with the old monk for the prescribed time and carefully learns each and every mantaram in the book.

Thick jungle. Sardiel 's traveling back to Uttuwankande when he suddenly encounters a huge black bear feasting on ants in a hollow tree. Angered by Sardiel's intrusion, the bear turns, lunges, and quickly wraps him in a deadly embrace. As the breath is squeezed out of his body, Sardiel recites the *mantarams.* Suddenly, he is all length and no breadth, stretching and twisting.

A puzzled bear returns to his meal. Flicking its tongue, a snake vanishes into the thick underbrush.

Sardiel's encounter with the old priest at Dikkobupitiya and his discovery of the magic *mantarams* triggers memory: three years back at the Temple school at Illukgoda, his teacher spoke of a certain magic oil called *heneraja thailaya.* The oil, once applied to the body, was claimed to be a sure charm against any bullet, at any range. The oil, it would seem, was in a secret place in a Temple at Badulla. Sardiel, oozing with a new confidence from his recent discovery of the ola-leaf book, is now anxious to add yet another magic weapon to his arsenal.

When Sardiel approaches the monk in Badulla, he is abused and dismissed—banished from the grounds of the Temple.

The old rage reawakens. He waits out the hours till dusk
when the Temple bo tree glows with a hundred oil lamps at
its base and the monk leaves his room to preach the evening
bana. Sardiel—a shadow blending with a thousand others,
then breaks in with the nonchalance of a cat, steals the pre-
cious oil and vanishes into the starless night.

The theft discovered, the monk raises the alarm, summons
the police and urges swift and grave retribution. Citing the
magic powers of the oil, he warns of dire consequences,
should the miscreant go unpunished. The police respond
with laughter at the paranoid fears of the Temple priest,
protest they cannot waste their time over a little bottle of oil.

beedi: a small, rolled cigarette
abitiya: young seminarian monk
lamaya: child
seth-kavi: a form of chanting
bana: Buddhist reading from the scriptures and sermon
hamuduruwane: Sinhalese mode of address to a Buddhist monk

The Bandit

KATU BAWA AND THE BANDIT: A BEDTIME STORY

—for Michael

Once upon a time, there lived a rich merchant named Katu
Bawa. Katu Bawa lived in a city in Ceylon called Kandy. He
used to travel very often to the nearby village of
Uttuwankande. This was the small village where the famous
bandit Sardiel also lived. The people of Uttuwankande were
very very poor. Sardiel often distributed the loot he robbed
from the Royal Mail Coach and the Colombo-Kandy Express
to the poor villagers in the area.

Despite their poverty, the people could not resist the
beautiful trinkets, glass bangles, sarees and cosmetics that
Katu Bawa brought for sale. He charged his customers
exorbitant prices and very soon almost every household in
Uttuwankande was in debt up to its ears. When his debtors
could not pay, Katu Bawa demanded the produce from their
lands. There seemed to be no way out of their misery, until
they turned to Sardiel for help.

One day, Sardiel heard that Katu Bawa was in town and
staying with his relative, Cader. Cader left town that same
evening on business. It was midnight. Using a crowbar,
Sardiel broke open the lock to the front door and entered the
house. Katu Bawa awoke suddenly in a thick sweat, a shim-
mering knifepoint at his throat.

Sardiel gave him a choice: leave town, keep your mouth shut
and never return to Uttuwankande—or else. In order, how-
ever, to seal the promise of Katu Bawa, he cut off half of the
merchant's moustache. He then helped himself to all of Katu
Bawa's money and much of his wares as he could carry and
left as silently as he had entered.

Cader's wife, who was in the next room, witnessed all that
happened through a slightly opened door. She said nothing
to her husband, as she sympathized with the plight of the
villagers and hated Katu Bawa for his greed.

25

Sardiel did not go home directly but visited many of the villagers who had been exploited by the greedy merchant. He gave each a portion of the money and a share of the goods he had seized from Katu Bawa. All he asked in return was their silence.

The next morning, a clean-shaven Katu Bawa complained to the *vidane* (village chief) that he had been robbed. Sardiel was taken into custody, but when Katu Bawa was asked to identify Sardiel, he suddenly lapsed into a strange silence. A few moments before, the merchant had seen a grim message in the eyes of the bandit. Frightened for his life, Katu Bawa left the village of Uttuwankande, never to return.

A BODYGUARD FOR MR SILVA

A leather suitcase. Three thousand rupees of his laborers'
wages in loose bundles strewn on an oval table. Mr Silva,
Ceylonese planter, packs them in neatly. Too late for the
coach ride from Kandy to Kadugannawa, he decides to walk,
though dangers loom in his mind like boulders across a path.
Sardiel in legend, in the air, possibly on this very road.
But a life of charity, compassion for his poor laborers, pro-
tects him like medieval armour.Karma and the gods are on
his side.

Dusk like a black fog now embraces this lonely stretch of
road; every tree and shrub dissolves into the darkness. A
bend in the road ahead: a slim dark man emerges from the
darkness, holds out a friendly hand. The walking
companionship warms. Conversation thickens. Mr Silva
breathes more easily, welcomes this pleasant shortening
of his journey. He invites the man to dinner, arrack, and a
chew of betel.

With half a bottle of arrack swimming in his head, a sumptu-
ous meal nicely done, the stranger rises and thanks his host
for his hospitality.

"And your name ?"

"I am Sardiel, Lord of Uttuwankande. I have been your
bodyguard tonight."

PLANTER DE SILVA LOOKS AT SARDIEL
AS THEY WALK ALONG THE KANDY ROAD

Twilight. The shadows round his eyes,
the light brown skin now darker
by the fading light.
A rather small, lean man, barely five feet in height,
is walking with me along the Kandy Road.
This couldn't be the bandit legend in the flesh,
the Lord of Uttuwankande?

His long hair, black as tar, draped down in waves
over his ears, to the nape of his neck,
to frame his face, define
the sensuous mouth, the hard jaws.

It was the eyes. The obsidian eyes
darting like lightning as if to pick up
every scent, every motion of danger.
And the cat in him. The way the limbs
moved liquid through the night air;
the language of animal prowl,
the cautious idiom of the hunter.

And as we closed the day
with a large shot of arrack,
he rose like a presence,
someone born to lead
and walked into the starless night
as if he belonged to it.

THE WORD MADE GOOD

High noon.
   The plantation   sags
under Haputale's mauling sun.
   Pure sculpture the bloodsucker on the lawn,
the rosebud
   a phantasmagoria of blood.

Siesta
   holds the Englishman limp
on his divan, his eyes folded.
   The veranda barely hides the servants
drooping
   like flowers in a vase.

Not for long—
   The master's voice booms
at a bare-bodied man
   standing arrogant
at the door, his rifle
   catching the rays
of an afternoon sun.

"Who are you?
   What the hell do you want?"
"I am Sardiel of Uttuwankande.
   I need 131 rupees immediately,
not a cent more or less.
   Will you lend me the money, Sir?"

"Yes, but why this exact amount,
   why demand such a paltry sum
at the point of a gun?"
   "Today, as the half-moon

crawls over the Rock,
   I need to pay my debt to Jinadasa ,
a poor villager whom I waylaid
   (at a point of a gun)
for my gambling needs.
   Sardiel of Uttuwankande
always keeps his word."

The bandit is last seen
   on his knees   bending over
to smell the roses.

Stunned servants crowd the divan,
   the head appu protesting:
"Master doing foolish thing.
Big rogue this Sardiel,
very dangerous man, too.
Master should call police."

Bungalow gossip
   hardly two days old,
when a hulking man stands at the front door,
   hands the houseboy a large package.
Rolled in leopard's skin:
   the Englishman's rifle,
servant's sword,
   and a crocodile skin
bulging with 131 rupees!

THE DOWRY

After the banana groves
now greener
    by evening's champagne light,
a clear road rises
    to meet an old man dragging his feet,
his purse tight under his ribs.

As the fruit bats
hail the gathering darkness,
    one weary foot
takes the next hairpin bend.
    The bandit stiffens,
his rifle nose glints.

"*Seeya*, stop right there.
Now is the time to pay your dues
    for walking the roads of Sardiel,
Lord of Uttwankande."
    The old man's knees buckle,
his toothless mouth stutters:

"*Buddhu ammo*, have mercy on me,
I'm only a poor carpenter.
    This here money
is all I have
    for my daughter's dowry."

"Stop whining, old man,
    you'll get your money back.
Meet me here tomorrow
    when the moon rides high
over the Rock of Uttuwankande."
    "*Amma*, why am I again

in karma's cruel vice?
Is the foul act, rolling dice,
    my life's dark prescription, greater
than a man's love
    for his daughter?

Why don't I see the cruelty
    of all this ?
How can the thrill of the dice
    mean more that the agony
of a poor old man on a dark night?
    What of *his* karma
on this lonely moonless road?

    The next night
a half-moon watches.
    Locked in the magnet of promise,
he meets the old man again.
    Voices break, then laughter
warm as the summer night.

    "Lucky girl, your daughter.
My *narasti malawa* helped me
    to win at the card game last night.
Here, old man, is your money
    and 500 rupees more, my contribution
to the wedding feast.
    Mammale, my lieutenant,
will now escort you home safely."

The old man said no words.
    Just sighed, then laughed from the belly.

narasti malawa: a charmed neck chain;   seeya: old man
Buddha ammo: O God (Sinhalese equivalent)
amma: mother

BEMINUWATTE RATE MAHATMAYA'S REPORT

[Extracts of a report to the government, covering the nature
and outcome of Beminuwatte's surveillance of Sardiel and
his companions]

7 April 1864

Sardiel, Mamale Maricar, Samat and Goduville Sirimala these
four combining together walked about armed with danger-
ous weapons such as double-barreled guns, revolvers of five
or six barrels, Poniards, knives and Cracklings. Having
armed with these weapons, house breaking and gambling
were practised by them, their relatives having lived along the
road at intervals from Mawanelle to Uttuankande assisted
the said four individuals as well as many other rascals of
Tanepene Pattu. As soon as these who were in the habit of as-
sisting Sardiel and his companions come to know of any
steps taken to arrest Sardiel . . . they inform it to Sardiel and
his said companions . . .
  They frightened the villagers stating that should any be
found acting against Sardiel and his comrades or relatives
that they will be shot dead; and there is no headman living
nearer than two miles to Uttuankande in order to look to this
state of things. Whenever a Headman or a policeman in-
quires as to where Sardiel is to be found, which only was
once a week or two some say "did not see in a month." Some
say "I saw him about a week since." Others say "I saw him
only yesterday but not this day" and so on and not only that
he could not be arrested by any Headman on account of his
having always arms, but keeps off whenever he knew that a
headman or a policeman is coming to his quarters and when
he knew the danger is past he comes out of his hiding place
and walks away to the house of his relations and friends, nay
to the town and go down of Uttuankande in search of bever-

age and that on all these occasions he is well armed and accompanied by his retinue though the inhabitants on such occasions meet them, no one would make attempt to arrest through fear, but they generally inform the headman . . . and by the time the headmen arrive they retreat to their places of safety.

The blockheads of these villages found Sardiel and his comrades and assisted them, whenever such a thing comes to the notice of a man of good character they move to another village. Besides which they frequented [several] villages for gambling.

In these . . . districts he had not lived more than a day or two, even that in disguise; also in the interval visiting Utuankande, such a visit having come to the notice once, an attempt was made to capture him. But he made his escape to his usual place of safety. His forms of disguise are on one occasion as a Malayan, at another as a Burgher and such like. He is only recognised by thieves and other blockheads, but not by the headman and persons of probity. He is known to these only by name and in fact many have never seen him before when arrested.

Sardiel had been to Coffee Estates too to gamble with coolies and to see if the bungalows could be robbed, which the owners of Estates were quite ignorant . . .

PROCLAMATION

TWO HUNDRED POUNDS REWARD[1]

NOTICE

Whereas it has been represented to the Goverment that Sardiel, Hawadiya, Baya, Mohamadoo Marcan and Samat who have either escaped from justice or are evading warrants issued for their apprehension on various charges and are all in the District of Tumpalata between Utuwankandde and Arenake, form with others a gang of robbers headed by the said Sardiel.

A REWARD OF ONE HUNDRED POUNDS

is hereby offered to any person or persons who shall give such information as shall lead to the apprehension of each of the other persons abovementioned or shall deliver them or any of them to any Justice of Peace in this Island.

By HIS HONOUR'S COMMAND
W C Gibson,
Col. Secy.

Colonial Secretary's Office,
Colombo, 13 January 1864

1. This includes the 100 pounds reward offered by the government earlier

GOSSIP AT CAROLIS APPU'S TEA SHOP

The scene: Carolis Appu's tea shop stands by the edge of the Kadugannawa Road that leads to the capital, Kandy. Barely seventy square feet in size. it has three round tables with nine crudely made chairs, all browned with sweat, dirt and dust. It's the favourite watering hole of Sardiel and his friends; they trust Carolis to keep his mouth shut. On many occasions, the gang would come in, high on ganja and coconut toddy, for string hoppers, kiri-hodhi and pol-sambol, *argue among themselves and boast about their latest escapades. Carolis enjoys the protection of Sardiel and shares with him a special love for the poor. Discount prices bring in the customers, especially the poor ones. For them, a cup of tea is perhaps the only sustenance for the day until the night meal of rice and dry fish, if even that is available.*

The house lights dim and the curtain rises to reveal two of Sardiel's comrades lounging around one of the tables. They present a sharp contrast. Mammale is larger, calmer, moves and talks with slow deliberation. Ukkinda is smaller, wiry and quick, radiating energy, impatience and volatility. They seem to reflect certain aspects of Sardiel's own personality. Both share the hardened look of veterans of a long war.

Mammale: Ado, Ukkinda. Let's have some tea. (*He spits out red betel juice on the dirt floor and bellows for Carolis .)*
   Ukkinda: *(with a slight frown on his face)* What's the latest? Sardiel *aiya* in trouble again?
   M: I'll tell you all the news, but *machan,* you'll have to pay your own bill.
   U: Alright, alright, Mammale *aiya,* you don't have to remind me. Don't I always pay for my own tea and *beedis*?
(Carolis enters and moves to the table. He wipes the sweat off his face with the hem of his shirt and then uses it also to wipe clean the table.)

Carolis: *Aiy Bowan.* What will you have ?
(Ukkinda ignores him while Mammale indicates tea and kokis.*)*
U: So, what's the story, Mammale, tell me, tell me. (*A ring of
black* beedi *smoke collapses over his curly head .)*
M: What's new, Ukkinda, is that Sardiel *aiya* has done it
again. *Miniha* is so hard on the rich folk, especially those who
are mean to the poor. You remember Mr Silva, the planter
from Kegalle?
U: Why, yes. Isn't he the one who was called *ratharan ma-
hathaya* by his labourers ?
M: Right! One night, Mr Silva was walking along the Kandy
Road when Sardiel *aiya* suddenly appeared from the shad-
ows and escorted him home safely without even touching
the suitcase he carried filled with his labourers' wages, three
thousand rupees in all. Now listen to what happened to
Punchi Appuhamy, the fat *mudalali*, after Sardiel learnt about
his lifestyle.
*(Ukkinda leans forward in anticipation—his lithe body a spring
tightly coiled.)*
U: What, what? *(Pulling heavily on his* beedi *and impatiently
tugging his earlobe with his left hand.)*
M: Punchi is something else. If a beggar comes to his front
door, he sets his dogs on them; he always shouts "No!" when
a *bhikku* begs for alms. And you know what? Punchi raped a
ten-year-old servant girl who had worked for him in his
kitchen. The man is so arrogant, he says the poor are God's
biggest mistakes!
U: So what did Sardiel *aiya* plan to do about this *vaysige
putha*?
M: Well, Punchi had one great obsession: a magnificent bull
and a brass-plated hakery to match. Take those away and
you have Punchi's broken heart beating helplessly in your
hands! That's what Sardiel *aiya* figured , and that's what he
used to plan his grand robbery. He's not just another hot-
blooded *chandiya* running amok, you know, despite what
some people and the police may say.

U: I know, I know. Our Sardiel *aiya* is a born plotter. Cold-blooded, I'd say. Like a doctor *mahathaya*.

M: Exactly. That's why his plans rarely fail him. I remember how he planned to rob the Nakoti Chettiar and kill him if necessary. He spent hours of discussion with me on what weapons , what location, what escape route we could use. He often broods on his projects for days, and visits the planned sites to study the layout of the land.

U: Mammale *aiya*, I know the man has more brains than brawn. If he was only muscle and bravado, I'm sure you would have taken him on long ago and claimed the leadership of the band, I might have myself. But you didn't, you can't and you won't—he'd eat you alive and you know it.

M: Save the idle prattle, Ukkinda. Do you want to hear this or not? There were two problems: Punchi's servants and his dogs. Sardiel *aiya* first struck up a friendship with the head-servant in Punchi's household. The night of the robbery he smuggled five bottles of arrack to his friend and asked him to entertain all the other servants. He also told him that one of the bottles was marked with an X—this bottle had some *kassipu* mixed in it, to induce sleep. The marked bottle was to be served last so that the servants would not suspect that the drinks had been doctored. By eleven o'clock they were all dead to the world!

U: But the dogs, the dogs, Mammale!

M: Ah, the dogs. At 11:45, he ordered Kirisonda to climb the gate of the compound. The dogs immediately began to bark and snarl and move towards the intruder—ha! Kirisonda looked like he might wet himself ! But Sardiel *aiya* had three pounds of beef laced with arsenic thrown into the compound. The dogs stopped in their tracks as soon as they smelled the beef—Punchi doesn't spend much money feeding them, you know. A few gulps and they were foaming and twitching and yelping like pups. Within minutes they were lifeless heaps on the grass.

U: But surely, Punchi would have woken up to the noise of

the dogs or the hakery wheels being moved at that time of
the night?

   M: *Modaya* , what do you think? Our Sardiel had arranged
for that too . . . That evening he had sent Punchi (as a bribe
from a petitioner) a bottle of the best whisky, brand that the
Suddhas drink in their clubs. As a taste with the drinks,
Sardiel aiya also sent a generous plate of devilled prawns,
roasted cashew nuts and some prawn *vadai*. By 11: 00 pm the
only sounds that broke the night's grim silence, were the
heavy breathing, hissing and snoring of the fat *mudalali* limp
on his couch.

   U: *(giving a shout.) Harima hari! (breaks into high-pitched laugh-
ter.)*

   M: The next morning, Sardiel *aiya* is seen recklessly riding a
brass-plated hakery with a magnificent bull to a village close
by. Punchi woke late that morning to a devil's hangover and
the heartbreaking loss of his two most prized possessions.
No amount of the cooling *kurumba* water, offered by his
abused servants, could ease his pain. Come, Ukkinda, let's
go. Meet me here tomorrow for breakfast hoppers. I think
Sardiel *aiya* is planning something for next Wednesday.

machan: brother-in-law, friendly greeting among male friends
beedi: small, rolled cigarette;   aiy bowan: hello
kiri hodhi: sauce made from coconut milk
pol-sambol: salad made from coconut
miniha: man;   mahathaya: gentleman
modaya: fool
Suddha: Englishman, white man
hoppers: pancake made from coconut milk and flour
aiya: elder brother
chandya: bully
kurumba: young coconut
harima hari!: absolutely right!
ratharan mahathmaya: golden gentleman
kokis: type of biscuit; kassipu: moonshine liquor
mudalali: merchant
vadai: a small cake made with ground lentils

SINHALESE BANDIT

Sardiel, a jail bird, and his 24 followers have created a great sensation at Kaigalle. They have committed the most daring acts of rapine and bloodshed. The police, it is said, are afraid to face them, as they are well armed and prepared for eventualities. I hear that the chief, Sardiel, has the impudence to write letters to the chief Superintendent of police.

The traffic on the Kandy Road appears to be somewhat interrupted as rumours have reached the cartmen that plunder is the order of the day. I hear that the Govenrment having taken the matter into consideration have offered a reward of £200 for their apprehension. If this little spark is not put down in time we may soon have another serious flame in the Kandian Districts. The surest way to put a stop to these depredations is to send a company of the Ceylon rifles regiment to surround the bandits and bring them to speedy justice.

Colombo Overland Observer, 28 January1864

AFTER THE ROBBERY: THE REVERIE

With cat eyes,
    I move through the dark house, stop
to gaze into the full-length mirror
    in the Englishman's lobby:

Buddhu Ammo, not me?
    A near-naked body
oiled like a fakir, ganja-red eyes,
    supple shadow of black flesh, lean bone?

Not me?
    Rogue, murderer, gambler, drunk
(as the *Suddhas* would say)
    mired and now mirrored in guilt?

Damn, what demons inhabit my body, my soul?
    I hear the hammers shape my scaffold,
smell blood, the Nakoti Chettiar ready
    for the killing, the glazed eyes
of the bounty hunters
    as their life blood quietly trickles away
with his bowels in his shaking hands.

I'm thinking of fame,
    how blood has its own flowering,
then the cruel illusion of it all;
    notoriety's false testament,
the mirror now telling me
    I'm no more than a near-naked man
with a gunny-sack full of trinkets.

What's left to argue, to keep?
    The karma of my birth,

a carter's son
    sitting at the back of the class,
a pariah with unwashed face, dirty clothes;
    my sick mother on a straw mat
sleeping away her fever, her evening hunger;

the poor widow   pacing
    her kitchen's dirt floor   waiting
for the return of the bandit
    with his gift of rice and dry fish;
Menaka's sun-gold face,
    her shapely buttocks tight
under a cotton-white *redda*;

And I'm asking
    what's the *Suddha* doing here?
Empire, greed, or bone-chilling winter
    or as some would say
those long grey days
    that smother the eyes, the soul?

He's now here,
    and the bugger *is* the sun and *in* it,
with a full-length mirror to remind him
    of what he's got,
what cold misery
    he left behind.

I'm hearing Cader's voice again—
    his argument of despair,
"Get thee to a Temple
    and put on the yellow robes";
No. I'll keep the banditry
    of my freedom,
my sure corridor to the poor.
Ah, the mirror, the mirror—

why, I'm still looking good, good
even in my near nakedness, my loincloth
   a white lamp to this darkness,
and who said otherwise?

My gunny sack's rustling.
   I drink to the poor, for you mother,
poor Alice Nona and her widowed hunger.
   Damn you, *Suddha*, you
with your khaki tunics and coloured marbles.

And here's to you, mirror,
   bloodless photographer
of victor and victim,
   mute witness to the Lord of Uttuwankande
in oiled skin and loincloth,
   to you, the oak butt of my gun!

redda: saronglike garment worn by women in Sri Lanka
Suddha: Englishman, white man
Buddha ammo: O God (in Sinhalese)

OBITUARY FOR THE NAKOTI CHETTIAR

The body of one of the richest merchants in the city was found in a cruelly mangled state at the foot of a huge bo tree just outside a Buddhist temple in Kegalle.The police were immediately on the scene, but have no suspects so far. The Nakoti Chettiar leaves behind a wife and two teenage sons.

Nakoti Chettiar, who lived in Colombo, often travelled to Kegalle and the surrounding areas. Well known to the *mudalali* class, the *aratchis, korales,* headmen, and most of the English planters, his name was anathema to the poor. It has been said that the *chettiar* loaned out money at exorbitant rates to the villagers, and often foreclosed their loans by taking over their homes, or demanding a full year's produce from their small gardens. Rumour also had it that the *chettiar* had been seen on several occasions in the Uttuwankande area. When an old villager, utterly distraught by his debts to the *chettiar*, committed suicide by jumping into a deep unused well, his widow sought the help of Sardiel to end the *chettiar's* activities in the village.

An eye-witness and companion of Deekirige Sardiel gives us his story:

Sardiel first arranges to meet the *chettiar* at his home in Kegalle. On this first visit Sardiel gets a loan for five hundred rupees and promises to return the money in three days .He pays up and then arranges another loan for a thousand, which he promptly returns in four days. Having now earned the confidence of the *chettiar,* Sardiel goes for a big deal: five thousand big ones!

Repayment date arrives, but Sardiel is nowhere to be found. The *chettiar* asks and receives the help of the village hierarchy and the police in his attempt to catch Sardiel and recover his money. Weeks go by with no results.

Ukkinda, Sardiel's trusted messenger, then hands over a note to the angry *chettiar.* If he wants his money back with full interest, he is to meet Sardiel at dusk by the bo tree just outside the temple. If the police are informed, or if he should be seen with an escort, the deal is off.

Nakoti Chettiar arrives on time. But Sardiel is nowhere to be seen. About to leave, an old beggar hunched in two, holds out a tin cup for alms. The frustrated *chettiar* spits on him and turns around to leave, when a kris blade flashes in the twilight and comes down hard into the *chettiar's* lumber area.

The fat *chettiar* hits the ground with a resounding thud. All over him, the beggar plunges his knife four times into the gasping *chettiar*, shouting, "This one [into the Adam's apple] is for the five-hundred loan. This one [in the landscape of the lungs] is for the thousand-rupee loan! This one [in the belly with a ripping and turning motion] is for the five-thousand big ones. And this one into your fucking heart for the old man who found death at the bottom of an unused well!"

The old beggar then plunges his blade into each of the *chettiar's* eyes, shouting: "Now, you pariah, you'll never see the village of Uttuwankande again!"

mudalali: merchant
korale: high, local official
aratchi: local official
chettiar: money lender

A BURGHER GENTLEMAN AT THE POLA

White cotton sarong
  lumped on the dirt floor—

The Lord of Uttuwankande
  now in Irish linen pants,
white Egyptian cotton shirt;
  my deep maroon tie
catching the sun like new blood,
  a gold tiepin (of the British flag)
preaches loyalty (or deceit?).

For jacket,
  I go with white English twill,
the *Suddha's* favorite under an unforgiving sun.
  Cool as tea-country mist,
silk socks massage my calloused soles,
  buck-and-tan shoes   glorifying
the extremities.
  Ladies and Gentlemen,
I give you the well-bred Burgher gentleman!

Off to the lakeside *pola*—
  with the crown of a summer straw hat
cocked at the right angle.
  Here, a throbbing empire:
laughter, chatter, children's running feet,
  the hoarse throats of the fruit vendors.

An old woman
  parades a toothless smile,
a basket of blood-red *lovis* flaring at her feet;
  sweet jakfruit in two blonde halves,
small pyramids

of sun-ripe tomatoes, mangoes, rambuttan
glaring in the noonday sun.

Then   posters   frowning
    like angry gargoyles from each pillar and post:

WANTED: DEAD OR ALIVE :
SARDIEL OF UTTUWANKANDE

A policeman walks by twirling his baton,
    greets me with a polite nod, mistakes me
for Mr Vanlangenberg, the Court Clerk.
    The magic of sartorial splendour!

And I ask myself:
    What is this *nadagam?*
Excitement, I say.
    Then, the luring of the quarry,
the thrill of blood.
    Now, the grand illusion,
trickery's empire,
    the laughter of the bandit
in a stolen gentleman's suit.

pola: farmer's market
Burgher: mixed-blood descendants of the Dutch or Portuguese, who
spoke English and wore Western clothes
nadagam: comedy
lovi: a small dark red fruit much like the cherry
Suddha: Englishman, white man

BANDIT ON THE KANDY ROAD

Naples is being cleared of Banditi, and even in Mexico the French are, at least, doing the country the good of shooting some robbers for the encouragement of others. But here in Ceylon it seems our great Coffee Highway is to be infested with a gang of bandits, while our police fear to cope with them and the arms of our Military are rusting. The credit of the Officer Administering the Government, is decidedly involved in the nuisance being abated.

No doubt General O'Brien was told that it would never do to employ the Military until the ordinance Civil Force had proved insufficient for the capture of this desperado. Even when they were at length allowed to arm, the Police failed to capture him, and from that moment the employment of the Military became the first duty of those to whom protection of life and property in this Colony is entrusted. The duty was not promptly fulfilled and we see the consequences in the deliberate slaughter of several innocent people by the spared bandit. Of course the families of the murdered people will be provided for; but that will be merely a duty performed by Government at the expense of a community having good reason to complain of the undecided policy which has led to consequences so disastrous.

Overland Observer (Colombo), 11 February 1864

THE ROBBERIES

(Sirimale's account of some of the robberies, from the diary
of A G A [Assistant Goverment Agent] Kegalle, 4 April 1864)

"From this house they robbed Major Murray's bumgalow. i.e.
he [Sardiel], Vederala, Malhamy, and Korale of Metnavelle
robbed the house, and Sardiel brought some of the property
to my house. I was away from home and he hid a double-bar-
reled gun, a pistol, powder and shot in a large basket of
Kurakkhan that was in my room. After my return he showed
it to me. The revolver was in pieces and he tried to put it to-
gether but could not. So he took it to a smith named Dingiri
Naide who could not do it. But he got it done somehow. I
know not from whom.

"I bought the gun from him for 20 rix dollars but some time
after Sardiel lost at gambling and he sold the gun again to
Gotta Rangkora, brother of Dolosbagey for 4. Rangkora after
told me that they nearly came to trouble; for an Aratchy
seized the gun, but he got off by giving 10s and at last he
managed to license the gun. He said he got the licence at
Gampola. I saw 13 bank notes taken out and I change 2 for
him at the godown and got 3 rupees for it. I got no more.

"After this, there was no robbery for some time. But they
used to gamble at the house of one Erneygamammana Ap-
pua. I used not to gamble. I never watched with the gun
as reported.

"After this, Lenohamy's house was robbed. I was present at
that. Sardiel, Mammale Marikar and I did that. There was
only £4 in money and we divided that. There was only an
umbrella and a tortoise shell comb besides the money, no jew-
elry.

"Soon after this, Sardiel and M Marikar robbed the Bengalee
man and the property was brought to my house. I got a share
for secreting the property. The property was for some time

kept in Allis's home opposite to Sardiel's mother's until that was burnt down.

"I could never get Sardiel to confess to Simon Baas's robbery. But report says that he, M Marikar and Samat did it. I never saw any of the gang. One night he, Christian and I were talking together and I left them and they were nearly taken. I complained to Sardiel that Gondewella Aratchy had behaved badly to me and he said I was no longer a companion to him and he would not assist me.

"Then came Samat's robbery of Henry Anker at Otooankanda. I was not present at either of these. Samat and Bardeen Cader's brother robbed the Anker's house. Neither Bardeen nor Samat told me, but I heard it from Anker himself."

SARDIEL IS COMING! SARDIEL IS COMING!

Like a salmon-pink veil, twilight lingers over this village for
an hour and a half. Then night forecloses with a darkness
thick as jute. Not a firefly, only one star, small and distant
gazes grudgingly over the paddy fields.

Punchi Appuhamy's big rambling house, with its huge teak
front door, beautiful hanging gas lamps, manicured lawn
and fancy wrought-iron gates, has been under the watching
eyes of Sardiel and Mammale for several hours. They plan to
steal the rich *mudalali's* most prized possession: a brass-
plated hakery and a magnificent racing bull. Dawn. And
Punchi awakens to a giant hangover, two dead watchdogs
and his bull and hakery gone.

On to the next village, where Sardiel's exploits are legend—
both famous and infamous. The rich *mudalalis* can hardly
mention the Lord of Uttuwankande without a crack in their
voices, venom in their words. Local officials would rather sit
in their kitchens drinking tea behind closed doors than en-
counter the bandit face to face. Here, almost every soul
nurses his fear like a wound.

Early news of Sardiel's coming flashes through the village
like a monsoon wind. The villagers take to their huts and
barricade themselves inside. One *kolla*, Zaccheus by name,
thinks he has found an ideal hiding place—the top branch
of a mango tree. The deserted village is now only host to a
single pariah dog lazing in the afternoon sun.

As Sardiel approaches, hidden in a cloud of red dust churned
up on the village road, Kolla Zaccheus loses his nerve, then
his grip and falls.

"Aiyo, Aiyo,"screams an old woman, bursting out of her hut.
She reaches her prostrate child just as the hakery draws to a
halt in the square. "*Buddhu ammo*, my *putha*, my *putha*." Her
keening voice is the only life in the village. Sardiel climbs
down from his hakery. The hard lines of his face now soften

as he bends down by her side. "What happened, old
woman? How did this happen?" he asks anxiously. In a thin
broken voice, she says, "He climbed the tree from fear, from a
boy's foolish curiosity." The old woman will not meet his
eyes. "But why? Why do you fear me?" asks the bandit in
some puzzlement. There's no answer from the bent head that
murmurs over her son.

Sardiel orders Mammale to take the injured Zaccheus to the
closest dispensary. As the hakery moves away, Sardiel
straightens and addresses the empty village. His voice rings
out in the stillness like a Temple bell; it echoes down alley-
ways, and hammers on fastened doors: "To me, my people!
Come out to me! The Lord of Uttuwankande and eternal
friend of the poor waits on you!"

For a minute, only a dog's urgent bark, a raven's guttural cry.
Then a servant of the Korale peers around the door of his
master's house. Sardiel smiles a greeting and continues to
play the town crier. Finally, the servant of the Korale comes
out of the house smiling and immediately persuades the
others to follow him; at first, a few, then a crowd gathers
around the bandit. Sardiel responds generously; he reaches
into his sarong's waist, pulls out some silver coins and tosses
them into the crowd. "Sardiel Jayawewa! Sardiel Jayawewa!"
comes the enthusiastic reply.

The Lord of Uttuwankande's conquest is complete.
That evening he leaves the village with a warm glow in his
heart and one more disciple for his band—the servant of the
korale; the first to step out of his master's house, his fears.

budho ammo: O God   puttha: son
mudalali: merchant
kolla: boy   korale: high local official
jayawewa: may you prosper

WANTED DEAD OR ALIVE :
SARDIEL OF UTTUWANKANDE

Dark and slim, her silk bodice
　　outlines the firm breasts,
　　her batik *redda,* the shapely behind.
　　She squints at the afternoon sun,
　　sidles up to the policeman
　　at the street corner, bangled fire
　　on her small wrists :
　　　　"How many miles to Mawanella?
　　　　How many to Uttuwankande?"
　　her voice thin as reed, the wind
　　dead as stone.

Policeman on the beat;
　　he is all law in khaki and baton,
　　puttees spiraling round
　　his short legs, his forehead
　　sweating the afternoon sun.

When did freedom ride on mimicry,
　　a foolish woman
　　with no geography, only dream?
　　The huntsman rides with memory, rifle,
　　the aching muscle
　　only after Sardiel.

As the *Vesak* moon
　　catches the black hair
　　coiled neatly at the nape of the neck,
　　the silk bodice
　　sitting snugly against her breasts,

the hills of Uttuwankande smile again
and go black with sleep.

vesak moon: full moon (that appeared on Buddha's birthday)
redda: sarong-like garment

THE WHITE ARABIAN'S FLANK

"No witnesses, Sardiel, no witnesses. Right? That must be the
key to our plan to rob the Arab horse trader. *No witnesses.*
Case closed, as you always remarked. We should lure our rich
Arab to some godforsaken place. The old *cabook* quarry not
far from the city is perfect. Dense undergrowth and the tall
spreading jak trees that circle the quarry would muffle any
sound of shots or screams.

"But, *machan,* what if the Arab chooses to fight to the death?
We have never seen this man before. What if he's a hefty
muscular man with firearms to back him up?"

I stare at Sardiel for answers.

"This is no job for cowards, Mammale."

Morning. A soft rain spreads over Mawanella. Ukkinda, loaf-
ing about town in search of the horse-trader, finally tracks
him down to the village *pola* buying some bags of poonac for
his horses. *"Buddhu Ammo,"* mutters Ukkinda to himself in a
flood of anxiety, "what a man! Tall, fair, straight-backed, his
rich clothes sitting on him like on a prince." Ukkinda then
conveys Sardiel's message to the Arab: If he's interested in
buying four horses and a piebald pony at a very special dis-
count price, he should meet Sardiel at the abandoned *cabook*
quarry just outside the city at seven o'clock that evening. Uk-
kinda also takes care to explain that for security reasons and
the welfare of the animals, the transaction cannot be carried

out in the village bazaar. The horse trader listens intently.
Says nothing to commit himself.

Dusk. The smooth swish of fruit bat wings overhead; mos-
quito buzz about our flesh; the air reeking of the pungent
beedi. With our tired backs against a huge boulder, we draw
deeply on our *beedis* as we wait impatiently for the horse-
trader. Nervous, I run my fingers through my hair several
times, shift the weight of my body from side to side. Sardiel
has that faraway look of memory: perhaps, Amma stroking
the fire under the rice pot? Menaka with her gold-skin face to
the sun? Sister Martha circling the kitchen with food in mind?

"Sardiel *aiya*, what's so sure about the Arab showing up
tonight? What if he read Ukkinda's message as nothing
but a trap," I ask.

"Greed, Mammale, greed!" he answers promptly.

There is something eerie about this night: the velvet dark-
ness; the faint echo of bat wings seeping through from the
dark hole of the quarry; Sardiel's unusual quietness, the
strange cold look in his eyes. It almost seemed as if he was
shoring up his energy for more than just a robbery.

Then, suddenly, he straightens up, turns his face towards
the quarry. With the ears of an elephant, he picks up the dis-
tant sound of hooves. "He's on horseback and I'd bet he's
armed," he whispers. "Mammale, let's not take any
chances. Let's jump the rich pariah without a word."

A tall sturdy man on a snow-white Arabian rides into full
view. Face, white as a pale moon, a shock of black hair falls
casually over his broad forehead; he rides as if he was born
on a horse. He's in white silks, purple cummerbund,
a glaring red turban on his head. Suddenly, from the deep
shadows, Sardiel leaps on the Arab from behind and plunges
his kris knife deep into the nape of the neck . With a pained
grunt, the Arab falls as his blood spurts over the white flank
of his beautiful Arabian.

Sardiel's on him again. Once, twice, three times, the serrated
blade flashes, finds its target. The Arab writhes and con-

vulses between his muffled screams for ALLAH. Then all's limp and dark and silent as the night.

But Sardiel rages on. As if feeding on the smell of spilled blood, he bends over and disembowels him, turning the Arab's white silks into a bloodstained winding sheet. Smelling death, the horse rears anxiously, neighs, and punches its forelegs high in the air. A shot rings out, echoes in the abandoned quarry. The animal staggers, collapses next to its master. Sardiel watches the curling gunsmoke disappear into the night air. He then discovers a wad of five hundred rupees among the Arab's entrails.

Frozen at the lightning speed and gore of events, I was but a silent witness. Such cold-blooded rage.The needless death of the beautiful Arabian. Was five hundred rupees the price of murder? Is the taste of blood an end unto itself for Sardiel? Has he lost the noble vision of his earlier days? I stare at my brother and say: "Buddhu Ammo!"

machan: brother-in-law, often used as a friendly greeting to a friend
aiya: elder brother
pola: village bazaar
Buddhu Ammo: Sinhalese equivalent of : O my God
beedi: a small, rolled, local cigarette.
cabook: a type of hard red earth used to make building blocks

WHICH WAY?

Mammale, my friend,

I'm somewhat confused at times;
things are moving too fast—
my feet seem slow
for karma's speeding treadmill;

when a man
is nearly hit by lightning
more than once,
he knows not only the meaning of terror
but also how suddenly life can end.

I kill, but I am alive.
They bleed, but I am whole.
One moment, a halo round a loaf of bread
I give to a hungry child,
another, a midnight break-in,
crowbar in one hand,
somebody's blood crying out
on a cement floor.

What makes love and hate hold hands
in the corners of my mind?
Look at my karma's prescribed journey:
Hope, the poor, the broken,
those who sleep with the rain,
who feel the *Suddha's* jackboot over their ribs.

What rage, what spill of blood, remains
in my troubled mind?
Where now that river
where Sirimalli showed off her mango breasts

through her soaking *idi redda?*
Menaka's tight behind
as she bent for the fallen coffee seeds?

Then midnight air, jungle darkness,
only mosquitoes about the tired flesh,
their thirsty buzz,
cold haven of loneliness, fear,
a lone leopard prowling under a broken moon,
my own placards of death
scrawled in blood, the white hunter
waiting, waiting beyond the treeline.

My brother Peduru shows me
his most recent sculpture of the dying Christ.
Talks of another way: salvation,
choices, forgiveness, redemption, love.
Nowhere the colour of blood,
except on a half-naked God on a cross.

Over there, Mammale. Look at that forked road.

idi redda: a saronglike garment, pulled up to cover the breasts
when bathing

Beginning of the End

IN THE BEGINNING

Mora-fruit raids   joyous storm
mischief   dirty faces;
torn banians   soiled sarongs
sermons in small fists
bond of hot blood.

Soon   gunsmoke
wounds   machete   flowing blood
bandit souls   one   with me
Lord of Uttuwankande;
nightfall   oil lamps
rolling dice   sweet toddy
ganja   laughter   havocking
in the cool den.

Among my band:
Sirimale, Mahamadoo Marikar
alias Mammale, Samat, Ukkinda, Nassudeen,
Moderatenne Henda, a dozen others.
Then an empire stirs,
the canon's rage,
Uttuwankande falls   grieving
for its fugitive children;

and jungle turns sanctuary,
life now balancing
on berries and rainwater
with only the voice of elephant,
owl hooting from the nelli tree;
and Sirimale turns Judas to the core,
my band scatters like monsoon leaves,
with only trinkets
in their bloodied hands,

and no one is left
but me
and my faithful Mammale.

THE COLOUR OF BLOOD

(Never wake a sleeping bandit
to serve him a warrant)

Past the velvet darkness
    of the banana groves, a clearing—
a small house
    with its whitewashed walls,
peaked thatched roof.

In the open veranda
    Sardiel's on a straw mat   manacled
to the angel of sleep.
    He hears   nothing
but the thunder of his dreams:

His mother, Pinchohami is handing him
    his life's grim prescription.
"No choices?" he asks.
    "None. You have to meet
your horoscope's dark truths."

The police party moves stealthily
    through the damp darkness, breaks cover.
A dog barks in the distance
    as if to break night's dumb vigil.

They hear Sardiel's heavy breathing,
    a smell of toddy and ganja
lacing the night air like a rumour

Panis Kapua, the police informant,
    prods the sleeping bandit awake.
"Sardiel, the sergeant and I are here
    with a warrant for your arrest."   .
"Is that the fucking sergeant's mother's warrant?"
    asks Sardiel, rage
shedding the haze from his sleepy eyes.

A jet of blood
    spurts from under Panis's left rib.
He staggers. Sardiel holds him up,
    gazes on the collapsing eyeballs,
and plunges the dagger once more,
    his bloody signature,
and another life drains away
    on the bandit's straw mat.

BY LEAVE OF THE GODS

Sardiel,
when imperium oozed
from each elwood helmet, khaki puttee,
black boot,
and the Kadugannawa hills cracked
to the searching bullets,
which way did you dance
to save your insurgent blood?

Did the *henaraja thailaya* really make you
immune to bullets,
the *narasti malawa* round your slim neck
whisper the winning numbers of the dice?

And when ambush tightened its muscles
round a certain Batticoloa mosque
did the *kalanganama* amulet
help you to walk unseen
through your enemies?

The stonecutter keeps
his long vigil in the sun
to tell his story.
You sang, as would the hunted slave,
a special song, long, mercurial,
loud enough
for every stone to pick up
the sweet thunder.

GYPSY SASTARA

Forest of distant stars.
   Cold dissolving moon.
A jak-tree owl hoots
   at night's grasping silences.

Long braided hair oiled
   black as crow;
night eyes of ocelot,
   a gold ring through her nose   catching
the flicker of oil lamps,
   her sinuous body
in lotus mode.

My dark palm hot
   on hers,
I await the oracle's story—
   fog of sandalwood incense,
silver bells singing from her shapely wrists .

The searching eyes ride
   my palm's faint and intricate byways
like a map, until
   a crucifix
of two dark furrowed highways:
Buddhu Ammo, she cries,
   then settles down with a deep sigh.

"I see blood   blood   blood
   coffee seeds roasting on a pan,
shadow   an old woman
   lying on a straw mat;
cold sanctuary of rock,
   solitude of the guilty;

I see a hanging rope against a darkening sky,
    the smoke of betrayal;

I see a Roman priest   hear
    trumpets of angels—
a man swinging   vanishing
    into the pit of the damned,
his body broken   his soul   soaring
    on wings of repentance to a god
who once listened
    to another scoundrel on a cross.

I see poor villagers
    their oil lamps sputtering in the wind

for memory.

Buddhu Ammo: O God
sastara: reading of fortunes

THE RABANA PLAYER

Rumour flares through Uttuwankande village
like a *chena* fire gone wild—
Sardiel's caught? The bandit's in chains?
The crowd's moving   moving inexorably
to the Market Square, questions
in their fevered faces.

Some—aratchi, headman, *mudalali*, policeman—
are already shaking with laughter,
expect the bandit's last journey,
through here to Bogambara Jail like a trussed animal.
Most, with lowered eyes, remember
their fallen hero even as they still cling on
to the karma of miracles .

The Square throbs. A brooding monsoon cloud looks on.
The festive *rabana's* in place, awaiting the drummers:
six women from the headman's household,
their victory fire already dancing
under their fat chins,
when a brass-plated *hakery* storms into town, pulls up
by the *rabana* players.

A slim dark man alights:
thick black moustache, gold ring
on each finger, a white Muslim skullcap
sitting comfortably on his head.
"What are you women waiting for?" he asks urgently,
"thump the *rabana*, sing, sing the death of Sardiel!"

Seated with the *rabana* players,
he then drums his fingers to the bone,
the *rabana*   resonating, resonating

through the hot humid air like thunder .

The drumming stops   suddenly.
The Muslim stranger slashes the *rabana's* cow-skin face,
rolls it on its round head .
Discards his moustache, his Muslim cap,
and fires a shot in the air. Eyes freeze
as he holds his broken leg chains
high above his head like a trophy.

Silence.   Dead as stone.
More shots in the air: comrades in the crowd—
lightning thunder   recognition   clapping hands.
It's Sardiel!   It's Sardiel!   He's alive he's free!
The bandit smiles the smile of the trickster.
Takes off the gold rings,
one by one from each finger
and flings them into the joyous crowd .

The harum-scarum boy from Uttuwankande Village
had not as yet finished his dream .

NOTE: My thanks to Gunasena Vithane for the story outline used in
the above poem.

rabana: a large drum generally used for festive occasions
and usually played by women
hakery: a light coach much like a Roman chariot
chena: a piece of forest land burnt out for purposes of cultivation

LETTERS FROM A JUNGLE HIDEOUT #1

Dear *Amma,*

I know how anxious you are to hear from me since I have
been away from home for so long. I hope you are well and
that the *varthay* in your left leg has now been attended to.
I'm sending Kirihonda in a few days with some dry fish,
eggs and rice. Be careful. The police, I know, are now watch-
ing the house. Kiri will come to your door in the garb of a
begging monk. Pretend to give him the usual alms of rice,
and as you do so, quietly remove the gift parcel from the
bowl. I am doing well, although I have been resting for the
last few days under this huge banian tree shaking off the last
effects of a cobra bite.
 Mammale saved my life. Soon after the cobra struck, he
killed it with an axe and quickly sucked out the poison from
the wound. We then applied the medicinal root that *vedama-
hatmaya* Themis had given me for such eventualities. From
here, I can see the faint flicker of a lamp in a distant village
hut which makes me think of home: the morning *hoppers* and
pol-sambol; sister, my brothers, their laughter, their stories.
How Peduru *aiya* learnt to carve those beautiful statues of
Jesus Christ for the church, and most of all their gentle ways.
I hunger for the peace that seems to ride their souls. Why,
Amma , did I turn out so different?
 I know I look bad, bad, bad, when you compare me to my
brothers. But never forget that I love you too, always have,
and always will. The world has not treated you kindly,
letting you barely survive on roasted coffee seeds, the few
sales of *hoppers* that you make to your neighbours.
 I only know one sure way to right these wrongs, make our
white masters understand the misery that haunts our
villages, the speed of a bullet, the knife's spurting blood, the
harassing ways of the guerilla. Now when I look at the red

berries of the coffee plant, I think of you and convince myself of the bloody destiny that I must fulfill.

Life in this jungle hideout is no *nadagam*. As if the nightly prowl of elephant and leopard, blood-sucking leeches, needling mosquitoes are not enough, I must also put up with Sirimale's stupid *Engrisi hatane* every night. I must stop here, *Amma*. I hear the distant rumble of elephant. Elephants in their mating season are quite dangerous. We have to break camp and move to safer ground.

Look after yourself, *Amma*—I love you,

Sardiel

amma: mother
varthay: arthritic symptoms
vedamahatmaya: ayurvedic physician
hopper: sort of pancake made from rice flour
aiya: elder brother
pol-sambol: salad made with coconut, paprika and maldive fish
Engrisi hatane: English songs
nadagam: foolery, comedy

SERAPINA BLUES

Cross-legged
    on cool grass,
I'm pulling on a beedi;
    perfect ring of dark smoke
takes to the mountain air.
    All's crooked with my world,
or so it seems,
    and now this:

brother Mammale   his adamant *serapina*.
    If there's torture by music,
Mammale invented it!
    Listen to the absent rhythms,
how the notes jump wildly nowhere,
    forget arpeggio,

compare
    the caw, caw, caw,
of rowdy crow,
    water hog squeal,
the jak tree owl 's screech
    from its alcove of silence
as if it were in pain.

I listen in chained silence.
    What else,
but my karma in stone .

    Beedi smoke faintly muffles
the *serapina's* needling ways;
    others squawk   squirm   spit
on Mammale with the red *betel* juice
    churning in their mouths,

71

but the shriek goes on!

Until he's laid out (without choice)
    from an ounce of *ganja,*
four coconut-shell cups
    of raw *arrack* wine.

serapina: a type of musical organ
beedi: small, rolled cigarette
betel: a leaf used for chewing like tobacco
ganja: akin to pot
arrack: a spirit brewed from the coconut
.

THE OUTLAW AND THE ORCHID

My mountain home   cave
bare as bones   fiercely cold

is not without decor
A single orchid explodes the darkness

Petals of spawning-salmon-flame
upside-down Grecian goblet

it bares a vermilion throat
breathes over straw mat, sleeping gun, dagger

catching an oil lamp's pale flicker
Legs folded on dirt floor

I'm chewing my betel like a goat
I rise   sidle up to my exotic flower

spit the blood-red betel juice
into its velvet throat

Lying down   thin black hands for pillow
I fall   into fitful sleep

The orchid still blazing
I collect the fresh blood into my dreams

LETTERS FROM A JUNGLE HIDEOUT # 2

Note to Mammale Marikar

Mammale,

Haramanis will bring you this note written in haste as now
even the mosquitoes are desperate to end my life. Act quickly
on my instructions. About a mile from your hideout there's
an old widow, Menike Amma, and her twelve-year-old son.
I want you to take them some rice, dry fish and a pot of curd
and honey. I also heard that she broke an ankle recently. Get
hold of the *vedamahatmaya* closest to you and ask him for the
necessary oils. I'm well. The thick jungle here is a castle of
freedom and peace.The moon was out today; beautiful but
moving, moving as if in fugitive flight. I miss the toddy and
dice games, you and my friends. Shall see you soon. Take
care. If we ever get caught, I pray that we'll go bravely to-
gether.
                    Sardiel

vedamahatmaya: ayurvedic phsycian

THE INTERVIEW

Sebastian De Silva must rest his aching legs. His lungs still heave like an old furnace. The steep rock-hewn route to Sardiel's cave up Uttuwankande Rock is demanding, dangerous. Mammaley Marikar, Sardiel's appointed escort, smiles at the "civilized" newspaper man and spits out his betel-chew. Cursing under his hot breath, De Silva resumes the climb. Cool drops of water from the face of the Rock run down the nape of his neck. But nothing can cool the blood-beat in his head.

This is the price of the story, he thinks. And what a scoop: the tale of a man who fancies himself a freedom fighter, lover of the poor, Lord of Uttuwankande.

In the cave, guns and knives of all shapes and sizes are neatly arranged at the far corner. A pot of rice is muttering in its steam. Hanging from a crude rafter is a newly skinned wild boar. Four oil lamps burn steadily, one at each corner. Darkness now seals the mouth of the cave.

A tremor runs through De Silva's arms. His legs begin to stiffen. He suddenly realizes that he is alone with two murderers, an arsenal of death around him. But the sight of Sardiel, on first glance, somehow shocks and distracts him and, in a strange sort of way, reassures him. He never expects to see a rather small man with a pleasant boyish face squatting before him ; it contradicts the legend of blood. But as the fire-light plays on the bandit's face, there are sharp lines around the mouth, suggesting hardship endured, determination and maybe cruelty; and the poised, lithe, well-coordinated body of a fighting man becomes slowly apparent.

Sardiel: So, *vaysige putha*, what do you want to know? And what do you expect to find? Does the colour of blood excite you? Do the khaki and spiked boots of the fucking *Suddha* frighten you? Since when do the "civilized" want to talk to the "barbarians"?

De Silva: Sardiel, your life story must be told. I admire all
that stuff about robbing the rich and helping the poor. I even
admire the way you handle the Englishman. But why the
blood and terror?

S : The murders, the bloodletting, I admit these. But there's a
certain karma about violence. Even the innocent, if they get
in the way, must pay with blood. This is life and death, *malli,*
an act that's often played out in seconds. Another thing, how
the hell did the *Suddha* take over our lives? Our precious
soil? Our freedom? With a kiss and a handshake or with
blood and gunsmoke?

De S : I hear excuses, Sardiel. Not reasons. Look what you
did to the Arab horse trader. You lure the man to some god-
forsaken quarry and murder him and his magnificent horse.
Why the innocent horse? No witnesses. No proof. No conse-
quences. What's so noble about all this?

S : Mammale, come here *yakko.*Take this arsehole out and
give him a good shot of toddy. Maybe you should also offer
him a stick of *ganja*—might clean the bastard's mouth!

De S : Sardiel, calm yourself. I'm only a reporter. Not a
priest. I'm not here to sit in judgement. All I want is the truth
about your life, what started you on this bloody rampage.
What sets you apart from ordinary men?

S : You want truth. Whose truth? Yours, the *Suddha's,*
or mine? I'll give you the truth. Enough to set your mother-
fucker's heart on fire! My father Adarsi Appu was only a
poor carter. Once a week I was sent to the *pansala* at Beligam-
mana to study religion under the monks. Most of the other
boys came from rich families, several wore gold chains round
their waists. Hypocrites. They laughed at me. I was only a
carter's son . They even went so far as to describe how my
father would tickle the bullock's balls with his toes in order
to make it run faster. My mother, who ran a small coffee shop
was not spared either. They humiliated me by shouting, *Cop-
pee, coppee.* I couldn't take it any more. So I beat them up.

Right there I vowed that some day I would erase all class and power. And the cruel *pansala* priests? Why, they sided with the rich boys! It was in those early days that I realized that greater power would come with greater numbers— hence my gang. Ruffians, all born to poverty and hardship. So you see, *mahaththaya*, Sardiel was born to be Sardiel.

De S : Sardiel, I understand your anger, your schoolboy pranks. But why did you graduate from fists to knives and guns? How did you end up like this, cornered like an animal, with the Englishman gnashing his teeth, vowing to bring you to the gallows?

S : Let me tell you when everything changed. Once, picking the mora fruit during the season, I was falsely accused of stealing a gold chain from a *mudalali's* son and was promptly thrown into a cold dark cell for two days wihout food or water. After this, Sardiel the *bandit* was born. There was no choice. I was already familiar with guns. I was a barracks boy at the army camp in Colombo.

De S : Alright, but what turned you against the monks? Why did you steal the holy oils? Why did you beat up the *abitiyas?* Wasn't it true that both your father and mother had relied on the monks to educate you?

S : True. But those *pansala* monks always treated me like a pariah. I remember my first day at school. I was sent to the very back of the class. Like an untouchable. They always sided with the rich boys. They never believed me. Hypocrites! They didn't give a damn for the poor. As for the holy oils, I stole them for sheer survival. They were supposed to have magic properties against all dangers. And the *abitiyas?* Those little saints once ganged up on me, gave me a good thrashing. Why? A carter's son should never be high spirited, never talk out of turn. So I evened things up a little. I doubled their pain one rainy day.

De S : Do you really think people will accept this "karma of violence" stuff? And after you admit killing the innocent, do you think you'll be believed as "the freedom fighter" you are

claiming to be? Sardiel, isn't the real reason for all your esca-
pades the excitement, the attention you get? As for the Eng-
lishman, didn't he just happen to be in your way? The poor
are just an excuse for your guilt. How come only you among
all your brothers went to hell? They too were poor, born to
the same father and mother. Peduru becomes a painter and
sculptor, Gabriel a quiet tradesman, and Anthony a teacher.

S: *Modaya*, think what you want. I've told you the truth. This
talk is over. If I was not a man of honor, I'd skin you alive,
and hang you up next to the wild boar carcass over there.
Sure, there's fire in my belly. And I love the fame. Maybe I
am no freedom fighter. Yes. My hatred for the *Suddhas* is abso-
lutely practical. They ignore the poor and suck up to the rich.
If they suffer because of me, so be it. Let the lovers of free-
dom clap their hands. It's the poor that matter. They are my
own, they are me.

pansala: Buddhist temple
abitiyas: seminarian monks
modaya: fool
yakko: devil
copee: coffee;   mahathaya: gentleman, sir

FOR THIRTY PIECES OF SILVER

This night—
    no moon no stars,
    no dance of fireflies
    or fruit bats with honey in their small mouths—
    only fog, fog thick as goat's milk.
In the Uttuwankande Cave,
    Sardiel, Mammale and I are rolling dice.

Sardiel aiya goes first, then Mammale, two others
   and I.

Four oil lamps leak their grudging glow,
   toddy and ganja breed raucous laughter,
   I roll the dice,
   come up with lucky seven.

Sardiel with animal eye,
   catches the flame of one oil lamp
   sputter and die;
   argues karma 's sudden darkness,

      conjures a black scenario:
      Inspector Saunders with a full complement
      of police and soldiers
      has surrounded his mother's house.
      But how did they ever know
      of his whereabouts?

He's already collecting the squealer's blood
   in his hunting eyes,
   karma's simple denouement? Or is he?
   He lowers his eyes. Hangs his head.
   Some other answers?
   A scoundrel's forgiveness, long shadows
   of the Judas tree?

A cock crows. His revery shattering like glass,

and I, Sirimale,
   blood companion,
   malli to my lord Sardiel,
   walk by the shadows of evening
   to the Kadugannawa Police Station.

malli: younger brother
ganja: local drug
aiya: elder brother

THE LAST DAYS

The capture of Sardiel—Sergeant Mahat's Account[1]

"On the 20th I went and told Mr Saunders that I had sent a
spy to look for Sardiel. I went (on the 21st) in search of the
spy Ookoowa. Four of us went at first—myself, Sabhan,
Hadji and Usoop. I and Sabhan were from the police. I met
Sirimale opposite the Godown (arrack shop) at Ut-
tuankande. I knew that he was one of Sardiel's party. We
went to Mawanelle. I saw Ookoowa there. Then Usoop told
us that there were two holes made in Cader's house. Let us
go and see. It was a tiled house. I examined the
holes. Then I found a doorway covered with cadjans.
    "We got into the back verandah through the unfinished door-
way. I went in first and all the five followed. There was a win-
dow. I directed Usoop to open it. I looked up at the loft (after
removing the cadjans and finding nothing below) and told
Sirimale to get up and peep. He raised himself on a beam. I
heard footsteps in the loft. Sirimale said 'there he is'—
jumped down and ran away. All the others ran away except
myself and Sabhan. I and Sabhan stood close to the cross
wall and stood there with our guns. I saw Sardiel stooping
and peeping over us. He was looking down in order to take
aim, looking up and down towards the window. I then shot
him on the buttocks . He fell down on the loft.
    "Then Sabhan shouted: 'Don't shoot any more. The Kandy

police have got the day. Let us seize him alive.' Hadji and Usoop went out into the road. Then Tamby (Mamale Maricar) came to the edge of the loft and shot Sabhan and he fell dead on my feet. Then Hadji again ran away. Again another shot was fired but the cap snapped. I then stood near the door way, keeping watch and sent Usoop to Mr Saunders and the soldiers. It was about half past seven in the morning."

NOTE
1. Notes of the trial of Sardiel taken by Justice Thomson, Kandy, 4 April 1864

Trial. Conversion

TESTIMONY AT SARDIEL'S TRIAL
—RAMAN PAKIER[1]

"I recollect going with Juanis Mendis, Police Sergeant of Gannetenne to arrest Sardiel at Negombo. I saw Sardiel at Polawatte. I knew Pasquel who was stabbed and afterwards died from the wounds. He was known to us as Paniscapua. He went and pointed out Sardiel to me and the sergeant. Sardiel was then in a house near the tavern. Panis touched him and said,'there is a sergeant with a warrant who wants you.' Sardiel said: 'Is that the sergeant's mother's warrant?' and stabbed him in the breast. As he was staggering Sardiel held him up and stabbed him in the arm. The sergeant and I were guarding at two doors. Sardiel also stabbed Migal who was with Paniscapua. I and the sergeant secured Sardiel. He then attempted to stab the sergeant and when the sergeant warded off the blow, the knife cut on the back of his arm. We ultimately took Sardiel to the Negombo Court. All this was at seven or half past seven in the morning. Sardiel was lying on a mat in the outer verandah. It was Paniscapua who roused the sleeping man."

NOTE

1. Excerpt from court testimony, 14 April 1864.

TESTIMONY AT SARDIEL'S TRIAL
—SERGEANT SHEIK PAKIER MAHAT[1]

"I received information on the 17th of March about Sardiel.
I and two other policemen went in the direction of his house.
Ahmet Pakeer, Abdeen, Bechi Naser and Muttu Samy—the
five of us went. When we came there, others joined us.
Ahmet placed me and another in the doorway. Some were
standing on the road opposite the house. Then Sardiel's
mother said: 'Haramanis, the house is surrounded. What is
this?' Saying this she went out.

"I did not see anyone follow her. I did not see the little girl.
While I was standing a mat hit my head. I turned round and
saw a hole in the wall. The mat was placed to conceal the
hole The mat I saw was being moved. I pulled the mat down
and saw the hole. The hole had not been made recently. It
was a small hole. The gun was fixed through that hole, I
didn't know by whom. It was dark inside . I heard one shot
at first. Two or three who were standing disappeared. I did
not move from my place. Another gun was fired through the
window where Muttu Samy was a little earlier. Muttu Samy
then disappeared. I stooped and went out. After I got out I
saw someone lying down. That was Van Haught dead. I saw
Muttu Samy wounded. Van Haught's step-father came and
said: 'you have shot my son. Shoot me also.' That was Chris-
tian.

"Before Christian came, Mammaley Maricar came out. I am
sure that was the second prisoner. It was after he left the
house that Christian Appoo was killed. Christian said: 'You
have killed my son. Kill me.' He was shot. When I saw this I
took two stones and struck the door. I told him, 'You have
made holes in the wall and shot people unjustly. If you are a
proper man come out.' Then I heard him say: 'If you are a
proper Malay come before me.' I did not recognise the voice.

Then I went to see Muttu Samy who was lying in a boutique. I and the head constable went to tend him and another went to see Mr Saunders. I don't know what became of the man inside. Mr Saunders did come that night and a search was made all over for Sardiel. Men were placed to watch all round and the Military were sent for. They came the next morning."

Crossexamined, he said:

"All this occurred on the 17th of March about Sardiel. I did not know it was St Patrick's Day. Our people don't keep St Patrick's Day. I am still a Sergeant, in Colombo. I came from Colombo. Sardiel's mother came and said the house is surrounded. She did not say anything more than that. She did not say that armed men surrounded the house.

"We were not armed. We were not sent to kill Sardiel. We had no arms whatever. I had no kris.I am not a pugilist; but if anyone comes before me I shall meet him. I told the persons inside to come out so that I may see who they were as a matter of curiosity. I did hear of the reward."

NOTE

1. Excerpts from court testimony, 14 April 1864.

A TOUCH OF LAUGHTER [1]

"When people were collected at Sardiel's house, I was present. I heard Pakier telling him 'if you are a man come out.' I heard the man inside saying 'If you are a Malay man stay there.'

"I am a boutique keeper. I sell hoppers, cakes and straw. (a laugh) I do not sell ale. If I had received the reward, the hoppers and straw would have been exchanged for cakes and ale (laughter). I went there with people who called me."

NOTE

1. William Nicholas Appu's testimony, 21 April 1864

JAILHOUSE CONVERSATIONS: SARDIEL AND THE FLY

Fly on the wall—
just as the cold cement floor touches
my horizontal back, jailhouse blues   call
for the *nibbhana* of sleep.

I've seen you dance, little fly,
north to south wall, east to west,
no steel bars for your rice-paper wings.
So why now here at my manacled feet
wiping your dirty little nose?

If you're here to keep me company,
what's *your* story ?
You sure must have one, one
among the karma of all things?

Tell me, little fly, are you happy?

Of course, I am!
I'm no lion or tiger or elephant,
but a little fly.
I can't help or hurt anybody, but
I can fly and luckily am free.

Yes. I've seen life
from the dung heap, outhouse,
mongrel carcass festering in the sun,
the dumpster's itch or
of rotting garbage.

But then
the unwrapped ham sandwich, pablum
on baby's fat cheeks,
the jar's open mouth, French-toast crumbs
on the kitchen floor.

And, those precious moments—
how as an uninvited guest at the Governor's Ball,
I danced on thin crystal lips   sipped
the sweet red wine,
and took my microscopic feet over roast pork,
buttered potatoes.
I even licked the Scotch off
a drooling, drunken soldier's lips!

Any scary moments?

So many near-deaths
from fast clapping hands,
lightning fly swatters, angry housewives
chasing me round the dinner table
with wet dish cloths in their trembling hands.
No love either from household cats or dogs.

So, why here, little fly?

Well, I had to see the man
whom the police claim is the deadliest of them all—
among murderers and thieves; whom others say
is freedom's thunder, the last hope
of the poor and the forgotten.

And who do *you* think I am?

What's it to me
who you are—
my karma's in my taste buds.
You offer me nothing, Sardiel—
not a single grain of curried rice or buttered crumb,
no sweet banana or papaw skin, not even
a fresh spot of red betel juice,
or minute scrap from your picked teeth!

So, here's to a cold bare cell,
empty hands,
squeaky-clean nothingness,
and here's to you, Sardiel,

for nothing   for nothing.

LETTER FROM PRISON

Bogambara Jail,
Kandy.
7 May 1864

Dearest Menaka,

I can't understand this. Why, only four days before I climb
the gallows, I should be writing to you when I had a whole
lifetime to do the things I should have done: written, spoken,
pleaded, hugged and married you. If there was anything I
was sure of it was my love for you, and your own deep feel-
ings for me. Ah, yes—but I chose the pariah ways of the ban-
dit (the Englishman *Suddha* would certainly look at it that
way), felt too much the pain of a mother and child sitting in
their small kitchen wondering when and how the next hand-
ful of rice would come. Why did God give us the poor? Why
the *Suddha* in a land that was not his? Cader would never
have married you if my karma had prescribed the narrow
and straight path. But, thank God, Cader is a good man, and
I hope you are happy.
    Sometimes, I fall into these reveries, and the old days come
back to me like the morning sun. Remember how as children
we picked the mora fruit together, laughed and called each
other names. *"Ura, ura, kalu ura,"* you would shout at me.
How we gathered the coffee seeds, and how when I once up-
set your basket of seeds you went red in the face and threat-
ened to kill me. You look so beautiful when you're angry.
I think I redeemed myself by giving you my basket, which
was much bigger than yours. And then, later, when I was on
the run from the police, how many times you and your good
mother gave me refuge, fed me rice and curry, and helped
me to go on my way.
    The other night I had this dream. It was an exact replay of

the evening when I met you at the well with a temple flower in my hand—and you said, "*Anay, Sardiel, aiya,* I can't. You are like the wind, here now, but gone like the raven." I miss you Menaka. I'll continue to think of what could have happened until the trapdoor opens and ends my dream.

Death is better than these chains, these cold walls, these iron bars that seem to slap me in the face each time I look at them. Nightmares haunt me frequently and I wake up in a thick sweat. One night I was shown a replay of one of my murders: the horse trader holding his entrails, looking at me with the glazed eyes of a dying animal and falling with a thud at my feet—a pool of blood encircling his body like a halo.

Don't grieve for me once I'm gone. I've now found peace and faith in a forgiving God.

Goodbye, Menaka, take care of yourself and give my love to your good mother.

Ma oyagay sadadara [I am yours for ever]

Sardiel

ura: pig
kalu: black

ANOTHER WAY

(Excerpts from Fr Adriel Duffo's report to Rome in 1864.)

"One day Sardiel learnt his prayers. The Minister Rev Mr Waldock, who visited Sardiel against his wish, arrived and told him it was hardly necessary—that good works were of no avail—that belief in Jesus Christ and an act of contrition were sufficient. That the good thief on the cross had never been baptised but nevertheless had gone to Heaven.

" 'Formerly' replied Sardiel, 'I surrounded myself with fire-arms and guns and swords to defend myself. Now with my feet and hands chained I have to defend myself against—that is the devil. For that reason I learn my prayers. Has good Lord Jesus Christ not given us this example? Did He not pray and did He not attach a value to good works and has He not promised to give Heaven to him who gave a glass of water in his name?' " [1]

NOTE
1. P A J Antoninus, *Sardiel: The Robin Hood of Ceylon.* p. 63.

SOLILOQUY

Ten more days, and I'll hold the dying Christ to his promise
to this good thief when the trapdoor opens and swallows my
limp body. This is the acceptable hour. To sit in this cold dark
cell and wake up from the nightmare dream of my life. These
prison bars that look in like windows to a life that has passed
me by too soon, too wildly. My galloping bandit days .

Dark nights of karma: the last cry of the Arab to his Allah, be-
fore I laid out his bowels on the quarry's red floor; how small
were my victories for the poor, how high the price. Cruel, the
deaths of Panis Kapua, Van Haught, those others who got in
my way. How the *arathchis* threatened vengeance, shoved my
father's head into an unlit oven; Sirimale's unforgivable be-
trayal; and Menaka, whom I lost; mother, who never lost her
unconditional and hopeless love for her murderer son.

Now, the soul's journey from hell to heaven. But before
heaven, Purgatory. Those dark spaces of doubt, memory,
guilt, regret.

"Why ?" I'd ask myself.

Who'd believe the sincerity of my conversion? Can a man
change his whole life, redeem his soul in forty-five days?

How would my poor mother feel? I remember how she held
my small hand and took me to the temple for *bodhi-puja* and
the evening *bana*; her quick tug of my ears when I blew out
some of the oil lamps at the foot of the bo tree.

It's not funny now. When my little sister, Martha, protested
my torture of the garden lizard, she understood better the
true meaning of *ahimsa*. I wish I did. When my brother,
Peduru, told me stories of the Christ, I yawned in contempt.
I wish I hadn't.

No. I didn't come to Christ on angels' wings. How my soul
closed its front door, fought back the intrusion. I told Rev
Waldock, the Anapabtist chaplain to go to hell. The good Fr
Duffo often saw me in the worst of moods when I wouldn't

listen to anything or anybody, not even my own broken
voice. Nor did I come to Christ with an empty mind. I read
the Bible, the small treatise on the virtues, the four last ends,
which Fr Duffo had left in my cell. Brother Peduru's stories
now made sense. The long, lonely hours in my jail cell threw
open wide the doors of my heart, my mind. And I believed,
listened to his voice: "He that follows me, walks not in dark-
ness."

And so, the soul's journey to heaven. Fr Duffo's Christ: love,
forgiveness, redemption, peace. Not karma, but choice. Not
blood, but love. Not darkness, but light. Not death at the end
of a rope, but eternal life.

I can imagine how the *Suddhas* would laugh from their
whisky bellies: "Sardiel accepts the religion of his masters.
Ha! Ha!" How some would shake their heads and ask: "How
could he forsake the religion of his birth? Forget the *bodhi-
puja* days, the *Vesak* lamps of childhood? What cowardice is
this from a man who once dared to defy an empire ?"

And I'd say: It's easier to kill an Englishman than search for
and find truth in the God of my masters; hard, indeed, to slay
the demons of my soul: anger, hate, the unforgiving mind.
No. Not cowardice. But courage.

In these last days, I think I found at last what I had been
searching for all my life: that mantara that would calm my re-
bellious mind. And yet, a rebel all my life, I go to my death
still a rebel. For Christ.

Suddha: Englishman, white man
bodhi-puja: ritual of sprinkling water on the sacred bo tree
Vesak: festival of Buddha's birth

ROAD TO DAMASCUS

And Fr Duffo led me by the hand,
took me past my burning bandit days—

past Panis Kapua draining his lifeblood away
on a straw mat,
past the Nakoti Chettiar, his bowels
in his trembling hands,
past that dark smoking night
in the abandoned quarry
where the Arab and his magnificent Arabian
screamed and neighed for their lives,

past the madness of poor Van Haught's death,
past the fading footsteps of Sirimale's betrayal,
past the spiked boots of my white masters,
past the sucking sounds of the *aratchies* and their kind,
past the hell of my condemned soul,

to his God, the Christ
who waited all my cruel doubting days
to forgive all,
offer mercy for revenge,
love for hate,
Heaven for Hell.

That one moment,
when the "Lord enticed me (with love)
and I was enticed";
when I, Sardiel, Lord of Uttuwankande,
trickster, murderer, bandit for the poor,
found for the first time in my life,
love without borders,
love   despite   myself

And Peduru's stories of the Christ retold,
the holy books under my red jail-cell eyes:
He who embraced the poor
with a love beyond measure,
"Blessed are the poor . . ."
Such music to my ears.

Another rebel, his against hypocrisy,
the polished sepulchres of his time,
mine, the *Suddhas*, with their jackboots on their huge feet,
their fat henchmen, the *mudalalis, the aratchies* ;
his Judas, to my Sirimale,
his crucifixion to my hunted days,
my last manacled walk to the gallows.

But He, a God,
I, mere mortal.
He, innocent as a new-born calf,
I, guilty as hell.
I die for my sins, deservedly,
He died that I might find love at last,
hear his words again to the good thief:
"This day thou shalt be with me in paradise."

Suddha: Englishman, white man
mudalali: merchant
aratchi: local official

THE FINAL HOURS

Fr Duffo's Account of Sardiel's last hours and execution[1]

"The fatal day was drawing near. We went often to see him to strengthen him in the anguish of the approaching death. The day before the execution, before administering baptism to him which he received with tears in his eyes, we asked if he wanted to retain his name, Sardiel. 'Oh, no,' he replied, 'it is too bad a name. It deserves not only to be washed but even to be completely erased.' We suggested to him the name of Joseph, the spouse of the Blessed Virgin, the patron of good death. He was happy with this name. We felt very sad that we could not administer the sacrament of Communion. Before leaving him, we gave him some advice how to conduct himself.

"He replied: 'Do not be afraid. If my companion wants to be the bad thief, I'll try to be the good thief'. This companion [Mammale] was a young Muslim who at the beginning had given us hopes that he would be converted. He had received and listened to us willingly. We gave him even some religious books. This reached the ears of several rich Muslims of the town and excited their fanaticism. They got a priest of their sect from a distance of eight miles . . .

"May 7th was the day of the execution. Fr Perrard was away and I went alone to the jail at about 6:30 in the morning . My first question was to ask Joseph how he had spent the night, and whether he had committed any fault after his baptism.

" 'Oh, no I have taken care not to soil my soul.' I gave him some advice and read some prayers with him. They brought breakfast and he asked me to bless it. He ate with his usual appetite, and what remained he sent it to those in jail who had shown some interest in him.

"Arriving close to the gibbet, in silence and in a humble but dignified manner he listened to the reading of the sentence.

Then falling on his knees before me, to the astonishment of all the spectators, he received the last absolution preceded by a short exhortation. He climbed the steps of the scaffold and placed himself on the fatal plank. I accompanied him and remained at his side. While they were tying his feet and his hands and were tying the rope round the neck, I suggested to him to offer all that to God and to join himself to Our Lord crucified. 'Yes, ' he told me, 'I am happy to do it, these ropes will become chains of gold.' Then, turning to the crowd he expressed regret for the criminal life he had led, and said that he was very happy to die in this way to expiate his evil deeds and to be an example to others. After he had said these words, they covered his face. He recited the acts of contrition and of charity, the Our Father, the Hail Mary.

"Then while he once more said 'Our Father in heaven,' the plank gave way and there he was hanging in mid air. But his soul was in heaven ending the prayer he had started on earth. Left alone on the scaffold, ritual in my hand, I recited some prayers, came down after being sure that Sardiel was no more alive. I have already prepared a coffin and obtained permission from the Government that he might be buried in the Catholic cemetery. "

NOTE
1. Extracts from letter to Bishop C Bonjean, Vicar Apostolic of Jaffna and published in *Missions des Oblats de Marie Immaculee.*

LOOKING BACK

to those taunting voices,
   rich boys laughing scorn
into my soul:
   "*Juk, juk,muk, muk*" —my father to the bull
"*Copee, copee!*" —my mother's soliciting cry,

   Damn. The silk of their banians,
the gold in their teeth,
   the *mudalali*-sucking priests,
the *Suddha's henagahana* ways.

   So the debris
of my rebellion,
    testament
of murder, gunsmoke and charity;
   the adamant fool in my head,
sudden regrets
   stalking my bandit days
like an evening shadow;

for beating up the *mudalali's* son,
   his head a heap of blood;
stabbing the Arab horse trader,
   the trophy of his entrails, the thrill
   of 500 rupees;
mugging the poor peanut vendor
   to feed a haughty mind   laughter
of 24 thugs.

   I am sorry— have been sorry—
for pushing the fat *korale* into the river,
   his pride wet as seaweed;
repaying those temple monks

by stealing their holy oils;

for stabbing the Shylock *chettiar* to death,
    cutting down Sergeants Muttusamy
and Mahat, the bounty hunters
    Nasurdeen, Draman Pakeer,
those two brave men, Christain Appu
    and P C Saban.

Perhaps I am sorry
    for all the blood
I cupped in my black hands,
    deaths waved like flags;
I never understood
    the British helmet and heel,
their strange voices,
    only the poor,
the hollow bones of their lives.

And so I danced
in a circle of blood,
    wondering about my life,
Uttuwankande's cruel shadows,
    God's flagrant mistake   the karma
of all these things .

Perhaps, yes
I should have lived like my brother Peduru,
    painter, sculptor,
who fashioned the forgiving Christ

so gently, so often, so perfectly.

henagahana: acts which bring down the wrath of the gods
korale: high, local official
mudalali: merchant
chettiar: money lender;   copee: coffee

LEGENDS OF FEAR

And so the dead Christ is buried,
a huge boulder rolled
against the entrance to the tomb.
The High Priest arranges
for guards to be placed there,
lest the disciples of Christ
steal the body at nightfall,
claim a new miracle,
a resurrection.

Now listen to this kaffir's story,
this man who was the Rest House Keeper
at Kekiwara, belonged
to the Ceylon Rifle Regiment
and was one of those sent to arrest Sardiel:

"Sardiel was tried and hung.
Then English people very afraid
his master bringing him to life again;
and they got twelve European doctors
to see that he was dead.
Then putting him into iron box
and making chains round
and putting deep in the ground
and covering over with cement "[1]

NOTE
1 P A J Antoninus, *Sardiel: The Robin Hood of Ceylon*, p. 67.

Epilogue

RECONSTRUCTING SARDIEL

If you condemn him,
     you're, perhaps, an Englishman / *Suddha,*
     a *mudalali, headman,* or a *rate mahathaya ;*
     policeman , soldier, jurist,
     or a hard-hearted son of a bitch—
     may be even a reasonable man.

If you praise him,
     you've seen the *cadjan* hut
     where a tiny lamp murmurs on the window sill
     and tomorrow never comes—
     no rice, no bread, only
     an old woman's sunken cheekbones,

     gnawing hunger, the boutique keeper
     standing at the front door   demanding
     his pound of flesh.
     Then Sardiel   his stolen mercies,
     his blood-stained hands ;

You'll also know
     the bloody stain of truth, history,
     tales of Molligoda's hot pulse,
     a cataplasm
     for Kandy's wounded side;

     echoes   Portuguese guns   the Dutchman
     gnashing his teeth at the city gates,
     how in the end, the Englishman takes it all,
     exiles a king
     and breeds a bandit.

If you understand him,

you'll know the real story—
his mother, Pinchohami's swollen feet,
a wrinkled mask
for a once beautiful face;
how hunger, worry, bends
her arthritic bones;

his father's bullocks frothing at the mouth,
    the long tobacco journeys,
        nights of straw mats and weak tea
        under starless skies, the smell
        of cowdung ever thick
    .   about his greying head.

How the temple-school monk
    seats Sardiel at the back of the class
    like a pariah, he
    with his dirty face and frayed sarong
    as the sneering rich boys
    stew in their silks, *havadiyas*
    and gold teeth.

And then,
    the wet stink of a jail cell
    for something he didn't do,
    how the anger of innocence,
    a congenital fire in the belly,
    moves the mind
    to the bloody daggers
    of the hand,

and a hanging tree begins to grow
    in Kandy's red earth.

Molligoda Village: centre of deep resentment against the British

Suddha: Englishman, white man
mudalali: merchant
rate mahathaya: senior village official
cadjan: dried, woven coconut leaves used for roofs
havadija: gold chain worn around the waist

SELECT BIBLIOGRAPHY OF SOURCES CONSULTED

Antoninus, Fr P A J. *Sardiel: The Robin Hood of Ceylon.* Colombo: Times of Ceylon, 1964. (Perhaps the best documented short work on the life of Sardiel.)

Cave, Henry W. *Ruined Cities of Ceylon.* 4th ed. London: Hutchinson, 1907.

Keble, W J. *Ceylon Beaten Track.* Colombo: Ceylon Observer Press, 1940.

Pippet, G K. *History of the Ceylon Police.* Colombo: Times of Ceylon, 1938.

Spittel, Richard L. *Savage Sanctuary.* New York: Liveright Publishers, 1942.

Vithane, Gunasena. *Saradiel.* New Delhi: Frank Bros. & Co, 1998.

Archives

Colombo Overland Observer (1864)
Ceylon Times (1864)
The Examiner (Ceylon, 1864)
The Catholic Messenger
The Sunday Observer
Times of Ceylon
Sunday Times on Web
The Island

Select documentation from the Department of National Archives, Sri Lanka.

photo: Jerome Crusz

RIENZI CRUSZ was born in Sri Lanka and came to
Canada in 1965. Educated at the Universities of Ceylon,
London (England), Toronto, and Waterloo, he was for
many years reference librarian at the University of
Waterloo. He is now retired and lives in Waterloo.
He has been widely published in magazines and
anthologies in Canada and the United States.
This is his ninth collection of poetry.